The Prince
Interpreted for Real Estate Investors

How Investors Maintain Power and Control in Competitive Markets

ANCIENT WISDOM HACKS

Publisher: NX Inc

Third Edition

Table of Contents

Chapter 1 – The Modern Principality: Your Real-Estate Empire

Redefining "State" as a Portfolio

Machiavelli opens *The Prince* by slicing the world into two basic units—republics and principalities—then spends the rest of the book teaching a ruler how to seize, hold, and expand the latter. If you strip away the crests and courtiers and look at the underlying mechanics, you discover a timeless operating system for control. Swap "duchy" with "duplex," "state" with "portfolio," and the parallels click into place like Lego blocks.

A property portfolio is a modern micro-state. Each parcel is a province with its own economy, laws, and loyalties. The deeds you hold are literal titles, conferring rights that the government itself respects because they are embedded in statute, just as a medieval principality's borders were ratified by sword and treaty. The rent rolls and income statements read like tax records, proof that your territory produces tribute. When you refinance or raise fresh equity, you mint new currency. When you write a lease, you legislate. You are both monarch and parliament, judge and treasury.

Machiavelli reminds the prince that he will be judged on whether "he maintains his state" and "keeps himself secure." In real-estate language, that means safeguarding the portfolio's net operating income, defending valuation against market shocks, and keeping enough liquidity to survive the siege of a recession. A neighborhood can turn, interest rates can spike, political winds can blow against landlords, but the ruler who lays deep foundations outlasts the storm.

The analogy even extends to geography. A shopping center twenty miles away is not merely a distant building; it is a frontier outpost. It must be garrisoned with competent property management, supplied with capital improvements, and connected to your information network so that trouble is reported before rebels—vacancy, deferred maintenance, tenant defaults—gain footing. If the outpost falls, contagion spreads: your lenders get nervous, your credibility erodes, acquisition opportunities vanish.

Two lessons erupt from this shift in mindset:

1. **Territory should be contiguous in spirit if not in ZIP code.** Machiavelli warned that scattered domains are vulnerable because the prince "cannot make speedy decisions." A portfolio flung across states and asset classes invites the same threat. You can own in multiple cities, but impose a unifying thesis—say, workforce housing within two hours of an airport, or urban infill retail on transit lines—so that your systems, teams, and data pipelines travel well. Contiguity is strategic similarity, not mere proximity.

2. **Governance matters more than volume.** A small but well-governed state outperforms a vast, neglected one. Ten midsize deals you understand beat one megaproject

that overwhelms your control structures. When Machiavelli depicts the downfall of princes who "lost their states quickly," he pinpoints disorganized rule. Your accounting, maintenance protocols, and tenant communication channels are today's equivalent of civil service and garrisoned forts. Neglect them and you lose everything—not to marauding condottieri but to lenders, regulators, and lawsuits.

To inhabit the role fully, picture a coat of arms on every rent check, a tiny banner flying over each address in your ledger. Your personal crest may be a clean spreadsheet icon, but it signals the same thing: sovereignty, responsibility, and the power to shape destinies within your walls.

The Investor's Sovereignty: Control of Capital, Data, and Relationships

A prince who reigns in name only is a ceremonial puppet. Real power comes from command of resources, superior intelligence, and loyal lieutenants. Machiavelli drills this truth with brutal clarity: "The first method for estimating the intelligence of a ruler is to look at the men he has around him." Translate that insight and you have the three pillars of investment sovereignty—capital, data, and relationships.

Capital: The Treasury and the War Chest
Cash is the lifeblood of expansion and the shield against catastrophe. You cannot dictate terms to a lender if your reserves

are empty. You cannot capture a distressed asset if you lack the down payment the day it hits the auction block. In Machiavelli's world, coin pays the militia; in yours, it fuels renovation crews and interest reserves.

Sovereignty over capital means:

- Maintaining an emergency fund that covers at least twelve months of debt service and essential operating expenses across the portfolio.

- Diversifying capital sources—equity partners, private credit, agency debt, local banks—so no single source can veto your strategy.

- Negotiating loan covenants that leave breathing room. Just as a prince ensures neighboring rulers cannot dictate his domestic policy, you secure terms that let you reposition assets without trip wires.

When Machiavelli writes that "the wise prince ought to adopt such a course that, if they believe they could injure him, they would not wish to offend him," he is describing leverage. With strong reserves and multiple funding avenues, you become the client lenders compete for, not the applicant they dictate to.

Data: The Spy Network and the Cartography of Markets
 Machiavelli calls intelligence "the sinews of war," urging rulers to plant spies in enemy courts. Your analog is data: rent comps scraped weekly, zoning board agendas, demographic drift, interest-rate futures. Raw numbers are not enough; you need

interpretation, the ability to spot inflection points before they appear in mainstream reports.

Build your spy network:

- **Local reconnaissance.** Walk properties at odd hours. Talk to shopkeepers. Attend neighborhood association meetings. Insights that never hit CoStar are whispered at these gatherings.

- **Digital surveillance.** Set alerts for every permit filed within half a mile of your holdings. Track U-Haul rental rates—they spike where populations swell. Use anonymized cell-phone location data to measure foot traffic before buying retail.

- **Macroeconomic early warnings.** Monitor Treasury yield curves, CMBS spreads, and regional bank loan-loss provisions. The yield curve inverted? Time to raise equity and refinance fixed-rate, because credit winter is coming.

Armed with early intelligence, you behave like the ruler who marches first, choosing time and terrain. You exit overheated submarkets while other investors still toast paper profits. You pivot to self-storage just as household formation slows. You buy loan notes before foreclosure filings become public.

Relationships: The Court, the Army, and the People
Control over people flows from respect, mutual gain, and the credible threat of consequences. Machiavelli famously advises that "it is much safer to be feared than loved, if one has to lack one of the two," then adds a qualifier overlooked by casual

readers: fear must avoid hatred. Practical translation: be firm on performance, generous when it matters, and transparent always.

Your court consists of brokers, attorneys, underwriters, inspectors, contractors, public officials, and yes, tenants. Cultivate them with intent:

- **Brokers** receive quick answers, clean feedback, and deals that actually close. You become their first call, granting you first look at off-market listings.

- **Contractors** get paid on time and praised publicly when workmanship excels. Word spreads and top crews bid your jobs at friendlier margins.

- **Municipal gatekeepers**—code officers, planning boards—remember you as the investor who kept promises: landscaped lots, prompt permit filings, community contributions. They reciprocate with expedited approvals.

- **Tenants** experience clear standards and consistent enforcement. No favoritism, no procrastination, no surprise rent hikes out of cycle. As Machiavelli notes, "men more quickly forget the death of their father than the loss of their patrimony." Protect their economic dignity and they stay, pay, and rarely litigate.

Beware sycophants. The prince is warned against flatterers because they cloud judgment. In modern dress, they are consultants who echo your biases, partners who rubber-stamp projections, friends who praise "vision" while ignoring underwriting gaps. Demand dissent. Hold "red-team" sessions where a trusted advisor must torpedo your best deal on principle. The practice inoculates you against self-deception.

Finally, remember that sovereignty is zero-sum only at the margin. Most stakeholders prefer alliance to conflict. If you can structure incentives so that contractors profit from finishing early, lenders profit from your low leverage, and tenants profit from long leases, your throne rests on gratitude rather than fear. Machiavelli's call to rule with iron is a failsafe, not a first resort. Use it sparingly, but keep the sword sharp.

The Mandate: Consistent Cash Flow and Asset Appreciation

Every ruler needs a north star. For real-estate investors it is mercilessly simple: steady income today, higher value tomorrow. Yield pays the troops, appreciation funds the campaigns. Anything that threatens those twin flows is treason and must be crushed.

Cash Flow: The Daily Tribute
 Positive cash flow is not a bonus; it is legitimacy. Machiavelli insists that a prince must avoid being despised or hated, and nothing breeds contempt from creditors, partners, and employees faster than missed payments. Protect cash flow through three lines of defense:

1. **Acquisition Discipline**
   Buy only at a basis that cash flows on conservative assumptions. That means underwriting rents at or below

market, expenses at or above historical, and vacancy as if a recession were declared this morning. If the deal still pencils, you have margin for safety.

2. **Operational Excellence**
   Once in possession, drive revenue up and keep leakage down. Audit every utility bill. Automate late-fee notices. Install water-saving fixtures. Small gains accumulate. Machiavelli counseled princes to study "the deeds of great men" and imitate their discipline. Follow the operators who produce 45% expense ratios where the industry average is 50%, then push lower.

3. **Resilience Reserves**
   Hold capital expenditure funds separate from operating accounts. Roofs leak, boilers die, laws change. Because you prepared, the expense shocks cash flow but never kills it. When tenants see swift repairs, lender inspections pass, and your reputation compounds.

Appreciation: The Expansion of the Realm
Wealth creation comes from forcing and riding appreciation. Machiavelli reflects that a prince should "endeavor only to avoid hatred," but he must "incur the reproach of meanness" if that frugality funds future campaigns. Likewise, the investor reinvests surplus into upgrades that unlock higher valuations, even if that means driving a modest car while tenants enjoy new appliances.

Four catalysts push value upward:

- **Income Growth** – The direct approach. Raise rents through better amenities, reinvigorated marketing, or repositioning the tenant mix. Because commercial property value is a function of net income divided by cap rate, each dollar saved or earned becomes fifteen to twenty in capital value at a five to six percent cap environment.

- **Cap-Rate Compression** – Buy in path-of-progress neighborhoods early, before institutional capital arrives. As demand for stabilized assets grows, cap rates sink, inflating your valuations. You win by timing, not by luck. Machiavelli says fortune "is the arbiter of one-half of our actions," but he immediately qualifies that the other half we control through "preparation and judgment."

- **Strategic Debt** – Use non-recourse loans with interest-only periods timed to overlap your repositioning plan. As net income climbs, refinance at a lower rate or pull cash-out proceeds tax-deferred. The prince who leverages wisely strengthens his arsenal without personal jeopardy.

- **Zoning and Entitlements** – Secure variances or up-zones that multiply buildable square feet. Paper gains become tangible when parceled off or built out. This is legal alchemy—a pen stroke at city hall can lift land value more than a year of rent growth.

Tracking success demands metrics. A medieval treasurer tallied grain and gold; you monitor debt-service coverage ratio, average lease term, maintenance expense per unit, and exit cap sensitivity. When any metric drifts out of range, probe root causes like an inquisitor. If turnover spikes, is it neighborhood crime, poor tenant screening, or a rent push beyond market? Diagnose early, correct decisively.

Balancing Today and Tomorrow

A ruler obsessed with conquest may leave the capital undefended. The reverse is also true: hoarding cash flow can starve growth. Set explicit thresholds: for example, distribute only 50% of free cash flow until economic occupancy exceeds 95% for six months straight. Above that line, you can safely harvest. Below it, reinvest or debt-pay-down.

Machiavelli applauds princes who "provide in time" and warns against rulers caught unready. Adopt rolling five-year projections updated quarterly. Stress-test each asset: What if interest resets up 300 basis points? What if insurance premiums double? What if the largest tenant defaults? Decide now which assets to sell, refinance, or re-tenant under each scenario. Planning is power.

Ethics, Optics, and the Social License to Operate

Cash flow and appreciation rely on a permissive environment. If the populace revolts—think rent-control referendums, hostile media coverage—economic pillars crumble. Machiavelli advises ruling so that the people "are content with his government." Practically, that means:

- Keep properties clean, lit, and safe. Pride plus security blunts anti-landlord sentiment.

- Offer rent-relief paths before eviction. Courts notice, neighbors notice, politicians notice. Mercy now buys goodwill later.

- Engage locally. Sponsor a block cleanup, attend city-council sessions, share data showing your renovations reduced crime. You craft the narrative rather than react to it.

Remember the paradox: to maximize profit, behave more like a public steward than a profiteer. The prince who appears just, even generous, faces fewer conspiracies. The investor who is known for fairness faces fewer regulatory shackles and collects rent in peace.

Exit Is Strategy
Finally, the mandate must include the method of relinquishing power. Machiavelli sketches how some princes lose their states through inertia. Your version is clinging to assets past their prime, refusing to pay capital-gains tax, or ignoring better horizons. Fix a target internal-rate-of-return window—say, once levered IRR drops below ten percent projected, list or 1031-exchange. Do not hesitate. The capital redeployed to fertile ground writes the next chapter of your realm.

Closing Thoughts on Chapter 1

By redefining state as portfolio, adopting sovereignty over capital, data, and relationships, and marching under the mandate of cash flow plus appreciation, you assume the mantle of a modern prince. Steel yourself with the maxim Machiavelli embedded in the text: "Fortune is a woman; and it is necessary, if you wish to master her, to conquer her by force." In our domain, force is disciplined underwriting, decisive action, and unblinking stewardship. Master these and the principality is yours.

Chapter 2 – Virtù and Fortuna in Property Deals

Prelude: Two Forces, One Outcome

Machiavelli divides the world into what a ruler can mold with his own hands and what crashes against him like storm-driven seas. He gives those realms names that still resonate: *virtù* for ability and *fortuna* for chance. "Fortune governs half of our actions," he writes, "but she still leaves the other half, or little less, to be governed by us." In modern real-estate investing the ratio feels the same. You cannot vote on Federal Reserve policy or conjure new births to fill apartments, yet you can train until every deal is a cold-eyed calculation and every setback an invitation to counter-attack. This chapter is the manual for mastering the half you control and taming as much of the other half as grit, technology, and thoughtful structure allow.

Part I – Virtù: Skill, Grit, and Sharp Execution

1. The Anatomy of Ability

Machiavelli praises princes who "have achieved greatness by their own abilities and not by fortune." Strip away the armor and banners and you find three muscles flexing beneath the skin of success: technical skill, stubborn grit, and cutting execution.

Technical Skill – The Science of the Deal

Underwriting is the modern prince's battlefield map. You must read trailing-twelve income statements the way a general reads terrain: Where are the bottlenecks? Where does revenue pool like water behind a dam? A veteran investor scans an offering memorandum and immediately sketches three stress tests: one where rents fall, one where interest spikes, one where cap-ex balloons. If net operating income still clears the chosen debt-service coverage ratio, the march continues. Mastery also means fluency in legal codes, construction sequencing, and tax strategy. An owner who can talk plumbing PSI with a superintendent in the morning and 1031 exchange timelines with counsel that afternoon is the ruler whose orders do not get lost in translation.

Stubborn Grit – The Untiring March

Skill without endurance is a palace built on sand. Machiavelli recounts how Cesare Borgia, struck by fever, still schemed from bed to preserve his dominions. Real estate delivers similar mid-campaign fevers: a masonry crew walks off, a tenant files bankruptcy, the bank demands an updated appraisal at the worst possible hour. Grit is the habit of steady advance through drudgery and doubt. It is driving four hours to confront a property manager face-to-face instead of sending a terse email. It is rewriting a rent roll at 2 a.m. because the initial copy showed rosy figures that smelled of fiction. It is pressing on when casual investors retreat to the sidelines muttering about headwinds.

Sharp Execution – Speed, Precision, Finality

Execution converts spreadsheets into deeds. "There is nothing more difficult to carry out," says Machiavelli, "than to initiate a new order of things." Deals die in the gap between decision and action, so the investor cultivates small-team agility. Letters of intent go out the same day a whisper listing surfaces. Due-diligence checklists live in cloud folders, ready for immediate deployment. Contractors bid from standardized scopes that leave no inch undefended by warranty language. When closing day arrives, wire transfers land at the title company before noon; sellers who savor that efficiency remember your name when the next asset quiet-lists. Sharp execution also means decisive termination when necessary. A half-finished renovation hemorrhaging cost overruns receives either a rescue plan by sundown or a kill order by sunrise. Hesitation is the tax that mediocrity levies on ambition.

2. Training the Modern Condottiero

Every Renaissance prince kept a standing militia of mercenaries called *condottieri*. Their loyalty flowed to whoever paid and trained them best. Your version is the constellation of brokers, lenders, inspectors, and managers who attach to a proven operator. The weapon that attracts top mercenaries is *virtù* in visible form—competence on display. Publish post-mortems after each project, noting budget variances and what you fixed. Host short webinars breaking down your cost-saving retrofit. Attend trade shows not to gather tchotchkes but to ask technicians uncomfortable questions about sensor calibration in smart thermostats. Word travels. By the time a complex, seven-figure reposition appears off-market, the broker calls you first because your name equals certainty of close.

3. Fail-Fast Proving Grounds

Skill grows faster in live fire than in books. Structure micro-experiments—a duplex in a tougher zip code, a mixed-use makeover with one retail bay—to pressure-test your estimates. Keep each bet small enough to survive but large enough to sting. Machiavelli notes that great captains "make themselves masters of the art" by staging mock battles; your mock battles are low-stakes deals where the only reputational risk is yours. Record every assumption, then measure reality quarterly. Where you were wrong, script a new underwriting rule. Where you were right, double-down next time with bigger capital behind the insight.

4. The Moral Edge

Cynics misread Machiavelli as advocating treachery. In fact he demands reliability: "The promise given was a necessity of the past; the word broken is a necessity of the present." Harsh, but clear. In property, a reputation for closing on time, paying draws promptly, and honoring tenant safety wins access to opportunities algorithms can't sniff out. Ethical behavior is a weapon; wield it because it works, not because it wins applause. The landlord who prevents rent-gouging during a local crisis may forgo short-term upside but secures a decade of goodwill with regulators and press. That goodwill often morphs into expedited permits, community tax incentives, or quiet calls from city officials about upcoming land assemblies. Virtue—small *v*—reinforces *virtù*—capital *V*—until the line separating them vanishes.

Part II – Fortuna: Market Cycles, Interest-Rate Tides, Demographic Shifts

1. The Shape-Shifting Goddess

"Fortune is a woman," Machiavelli warns, "and if you wish to keep her under it is necessary to beat and ill-use her." His language is medieval; the lesson timeless: luck favors the audacious but punishes the unprepared. In real estate, raw fortune arrives packaged as macro forces too big for any one investor to bend outright. The trick is to know when to lean with the gust and when to brace against it.

2. Market Cycles – The Four Seasons of Value

Property markets move through the widely studied stages of recovery, expansion, hypersupply, and recession. Each phase rearranges risk and reward.

Recovery is the thaw. Vacancies remain high, rents flat, but private capital has not yet returned. The investor with courage and cash harvests bargains nobody else wants—brownfields, half-empty Class C offices ripe for loft conversions.

Expansion blossoms next. Employment rises, absorption outpaces deliveries, and equity fountains flow. Class A builds pre-lease at dizzying rates. Here the wise owner sells non-core assets at frothy caps, harvests gains, and stockpiles reserves.

Hypersupply appears when cranes dominate skylines and leasing agents offer signed baseball bats to tour. New inventory exceeds demand; concessions balloon. The prince who hoarded cash now cherry-picks loan notes from nervous builders on the brink.

Recession bites last. Rentals dip, cap rates decompress, but construction stops. This winter prunes the forest so recovery can sprout again. The disciplined investor, still liquid, absorbs distressed portfolios at basis levels the prior cycle deemed impossible.

Recognizing the season is half craft, half feeling—absorption numbers, yes, but also broker small talk and the length of lender committees. Track both.

3. Interest-Rate Tides – The Pulse Beneath the Sand

Rates dictate leverage terms, exit caps, and buyer psychology. A one-point spike in the ten-year Treasury can vaporize millions in convexity for a levered portfolio. Machiavelli writes that princes must "build such foundations that when adversity comes, they are prepared." Translation: Use fixed-rate or capped-rate debt when policy loose talk grows hawkish. Ladder maturities so no calendar year holds more principal due than free cash flow can reasonably amortize. Cultivate relationships with credit unions and life-co lenders whose pricing mechanisms differ from securitized debt; their appetite may remain when CMBS shuts.

Interest rates also reveal opportunity. Rapid hikes freeze weaker hands; refinancing risk becomes distress you can rescue—at a price that honors your cushion. A prince surveying war-shocked lands chooses strongholds cheap; an investor buys notes at 60 cents on the dollar, then works with borrowers or forecloses responsibly, emerging with basis impossible in calmer times.

4. Demographic Shifts – The March of Crowds

People carry rents in their pockets. Track where they go, how they age, what they crave. Millennials sought downtown walkability and poured heat into urban multifamily; Gen Z shows equal appetite for "15-minute suburb" formats combining lower cost with curated retail pods. Retiring Boomers unload McMansions and rent in 55-plus, single-story communities. Immigration pulses into "gateway" metros then diffuses to secondary cities when rents soar. Each wave redraws demand maps.

Demographic fortune hands windfall to the early settler. Buy land along secondary rail corridors before urban planners christen "innovation districts." Accumulate garden apartments on the interstate ring where logistics outfits sprout warehouses; blue-collar tenants follow the jobs. When an employer announces a thousand-person relocation, race to tie up land for workforce housing before consultants can print their first slide deck. Machiavelli praises princes who anticipate "changes of fortune and meet them vigorously." Meeting demographics vigorously means deeds recorded before pundits coin a catchy nickname for the neighborhood.

5. Black Swans, Gray Rhinos, and Other Beasts

Not every gust fits neatly into cyclical charts. A pandemic shutters offices worldwide, telework becomes culture, Class A vacancy spikes in CBDs while suburban housing ignites. A regional bank panic tightens credit overnight, punishing developers mid-draw.

Political upheaval passes rent caps that slash NOI on asset classes once deemed bulletproof. These are fortune's ambushes.

Preparation still matters. Hold tax records showing median incomes for each asset's radius; you will know instantly whose rent relief requests ring legitimate. Maintain vendor lists in multiple states; if one governor forbids construction for months, you can shift renovation capital to jurisdictions still open. Keep an in-house counsel or retainer ready to parse emergency laws before they become headlines. Black swans stay black only to those without radar.

Part III – Systems to Tilt Fortune Your Way

If fortune rules half the board, systems are your knights and rooks—pieces designed to maneuver quickly, block attack, and exploit openings. Three categories offer leverage: data analytics, optionality, and liquidity buffers.

1. Data Analytics – Your Invisible Spy Network

Machiavelli recommended actual spies. Your digital age equivalent is a multilayered analytics stack.

Market-Level Dashboards
 Feed real-time feeds: MLS, STR platforms, public transit counts, crime blotters scraped nightly. Overlay on GIS maps. Flag ZIP codes where rent increases exceed wage growth by two standard deviations; such tension precedes either legislation or out-migration—both signals to tread carefully or prepare advocacy.

Asset-Level Sensors
 IoT meters stream water, gas, and electric data hourly. Sudden spikes trigger maintenance dispatch before tenants notice, slashing surprise expenses. Temperature variance in a unit can betray unauthorized occupancy; software pings management for follow-up.

Predictive Algorithms
 Machine-learning models trained on vacancies predict renewal probability by tenant cohort. Offer early concessions to high-value but flight-risk residents, boosting retention without blanket discounts. Feed leasing data back into model; the loop tightens.

Analytics spin fortune's fog into probability maps. You will never know the future, but you will know what it is *likely* to do in time to reposition.

2. Optionality – Designs for Multiple Futures

A rigid plan snaps under stress; a flexible deal bends and rebounds. Optionality is architecture that embeds exit ramps and alternate uses.

Capital Stack Flexibility
 Pair senior debt with mezzanine that automatically converts to preferred equity if DSCR drops below threshold, averting technical default. Insert earn-out clauses letting you tap additional loan proceeds when NOI milestones hit, instead of refinancing mid-cycle.

Physical Convertibility
 Purchase shell retail bays with demising walls pre-engineered to reformat as co-working or micro-storage. Secure zoning variances

upfront for hospitality use, even if initial model is traditional multifamily; a travel-demand boom could triple gross revenue.

Exit Strategy Tiers
 Underwrite every acquisition four ways: long-term hold, value-add sale year five, condo conversion, and fractional sale of air rights. Track quarterly which path now offers superior risk-adjusted yield. Sell, hold, or repurpose without losing time in new feasibility studies.

Optionality means fortune can blow hot, cold, or sideways and you remain seller of a relevant product. Machiavelli advised princes to build fortresses but also maintain roads for rapid retreat; optionality is your reinforced gate *and* your secret tunnel.

3. Liquidity Buffers – The War Chest Reloaded

When enemies breach walls, coin buys replacement troops. In property, cash covers loan covenants, cap-ex, and opportunity snatching. Liquidity comes in layers.

Operating Reserves
 Segregated accounts equal to at least six months of operating expenses and debt service per asset. Digital dashboards show burn rate in real time; red lights flash when reserves slip below target.

Undrawn Credit Lines
 Maintain revolving facilities secured by stabilized properties. Negotiate commitment fees low enough to tolerate idle capacity; the mere existence calms lenders during macro tremors.

Dry-Powder Equity
Cultivate partners who commit capital without deal identified.
Document triggers—yield thresholds, asset class limits—so funds
deploy within days of notice. These alliances mirror Renaissance
pledges where neighboring dukes promised troops on call; they
materialize only if relationships were cultivated years prior.

Liquidity buffers do more than defend; they attack. Distress rarely
waits; auctions close in weeks. The investor who wires earnest
money same day seizes assets while rivals scramble to syndicate.

4. Governance Loops – Turning Systems into Habit

A tool unused is rust. Schedule standing "state of the principality"
reviews each quarter. Present dashboards, reserve balances,
optionality status. Assign red, yellow, green flags. Escalate red
items to same-day action: fund reserves, trigger asset sale,
renegotiate loan covenants. Yellow items earn ninety-day plans.
Green items get a nod and return to watch-list.

Machiavelli counseled that a ruler "must read histories and reflect
on the deeds of great men" to adapt. Your governance loop
rereads your own story—metrics recorded, variances logged—so
next quarter's moves emerge from evidence, not ego.

Epilogue: Weaving Virtù and Fortuna

Skill draws the bow, grit holds it steady, execution looses the
arrow. Wind may sway the shaft but advanced scouting,
adjustable fletching, and spare quivers ensure enough arrows

strike. *Virtù* without *fortuna* is a genius architect designing castles in drought-stricken deserts; *fortuna* without *virtù* is lotto winnings spent on baubles. Together they build an empire.

Hold on to Machiavelli's final challenge: "I conclude therefore that fortune being changeful and mankind steadfast in their ways, so long as the two are in agreement men are successful, but when they fall out men fail." Your mission is to remain changeful where it counts—systems, options, cash—yet steadfast in pursuit of excellence. Do that, and no cycle, rate shock, or demographic upheaval can erase the dominion you carve, one deed recording at a time.

Chapter 3 – Conquest vs. Inheritance: Entry Strategies

Prologue: Two Doors Into the Kingdom

Machiavelli begins *The Prince* by dividing realms into those a ruler inherits and those he seizes. "There are hereditary states," he writes, "and new principalities." The same split cleaves the real-estate world. Some assets come to an investor already humming, leased, and lender-approved—modern heirs to hereditary dukedoms. Others are wrested from chaos—vacant, neglected, or hidden from public view—territories won by storming gates at dawn. Each path demands a different temperament, capital stack, and investigative lens. Walk through the wrong door unprepared and the very victory will ruin you. Choose wisely, prepare relentlessly, and you can toggle between the strategies as cycles shift, compounding wealth through alternating seasons of ease and audacity.

Part I – "Inheritance": Turnkey Rentals and Stabilized Assets

1. The Nature of the Inherited Principality

Machiavelli remarks that hereditary states "are accustomed to live under a prince" and therefore cling naturally to familiar rule. In property terms, a stabilized asset is trained to obey: rents arrive on schedule, expenses follow predictable rhythms, and maintenance logs read like clockwork. Cash flow is the daily tribute proving the realm's order. You, the incoming owner, step into regalia already tailored—leases inked, lender covenants satisfied, tax assessments current.

Typical examples:

- A garden-style apartment complex built fifteen years ago, currently 95 percent occupied, with staggered leases and a professional manager in place.

- A single-tenant net-lease retail box where a national pharmacy brand pays all operating expenses and still has nine years remaining on the term.

- A portfolio of small industrial condos, each unit sold to long-term craft-manufacturing tenants but governed by a master association that maintains shared roofs and paving.

The charm of inheritance is visible on day one: yield you can model with bankerly confidence, headaches outsourced to existing staff, and a path to refinancing at compressed spreads because lenders adore stability. Yet within that tranquility lurks the danger Machiavelli warns against: complacency. "Such princes," he says of heirs, "have less cause and less necessity to offend…" but if they "give way to evil," the state will rebel. Neglect a boiler, ignore deferred cap-ex, treat tenants as an afterthought, and the realm you bought precisely for its steadiness will defect, one lease at a time.

2. Strategic Objectives for Heirs

Your mission in an inherited play is twofold: protect the moat and widen it. Protection means preserving occupancy and margins; widening means squeezing inefficiency from operations or unlocking ancillary income without disrupting tenant goodwill. Think tightened utility audits, renegotiated service contracts, or adding tech amenities that justify incremental rent bumps. The paradox is that every improvement must feel seamless; tenants signed up for predictability. They will not applaud dramatic changes that smell like conquest. Instead, they reward subtle upward tweaks—a faster maintenance response powered by app-based tickets, a security upgrade finished in a single weekend, landscaping that blooms earlier in spring and is gone by first frost in fall.

3. The Due-Diligence Playbook for Turnkey Deals

A. Financial Autopsy
 Start with trailing-twelve operating statements, but do not trust them until reconciled back to tax returns and bank statements. Compare vendor line items across three years; a sudden drop in snow removal costs may signal an owner who skimped the previous winter. Calculate a *pro forma* reserve for replacement even if the seller's numbers omit it. Underwrite the deal twice—once at the provided expenses and once with a stress-tested expense ratio; accept the lower of the two resulting valuations. Remember Machiavelli's counsel: "The prince ought to have no other aim or thought, nor select anything else for his

study, than war and its rules." Your war is ensuring the revenue fortress truly stands.

B. Lease File Reconnaissance

Demand estoppel certificates from major tenants and spot-check five random residential leases for hidden concessions or verbal side deals. Scrutinize any clause granting renewal options at fixed rents far below projected market. An heir who inherits such poison pills finds his royal income capped while expenses march upward.

C. Physical Inspection

Stabilized is not the same as pristine. Hire mechanical, structural, and environmental specialists. They should crawl the roof deck, snake the sewer lines, and thermal-scan electrical panels. If a seller balks at intrusive inspection, walk away; the refusal signals an aristocrat with secrets best left buried.

D. Management Culture Assessment

Meet onsite staff alone, without ownership present. Ask frontline technicians what budget approvals look like, how often training occurs, and what repair backlog keeps them awake. Body language reveals morale. In a hereditary state the bureaucracy is your inheritance; if it is bloated or resentful, you are buying a rebellion in disguise.

E. Legal and Regulatory Review

Confirm zoning compliance, special-use permits, ADA adherence, and any late-night noise citations. A property can cash-flow like a mint until a city inspector catches outdated fire egress signage and slaps on daily fines.

F. Integration Blueprint

Draft a ninety-day takeover plan before closing. Assign

responsibility for transition notices, vendor payments, and software conversions. Tenants should experience zero confusion on the rent-due date after title changes. Machiavelli says hereditary subjects cling to a prince "so long as he does not depart from the customs of his ancestors." Your ancestors are the prior owner's systems; mirror them first, improve them later.

Part II – "Conquest": Distressed, Off-Market, and Value-Add

1. The Nature of the New Principality

"Men fish with line, not with nets," Machiavelli observes, "for he who would seize much loses all." Conquest deals are the single lines you cast into murky water: maybe you hook treasure, maybe a rusted tire. These assets resist acquisition—vacant warehouses without climate control; boarded triplexes the bank dropped from its REO list; mom-and-pop motels inherited by heirs who can't agree whether to sell or bulldoze. Off-market opportunities often appear through whispered introductions because listing them would expose messy legal or physical realities.

Value-add plays are a subset of conquest where the bones are sound but underused: a midrise with tiny kitchens crying for open-plan rehab, a storage facility missing contactless gates, a suburban strip center 60 percent occupied only because signage dates from the Clinton administration. Here victory lies not in taking possession—that part is the prologue—but in remaking the territory so its people (tenants, lenders, neighbors) recognize new value.

2. The Mindset of the Conqueror

Machiavelli warns that a prince seizing new lands "always finds enemies in all those who have been offended by his new rule." For the investor, those enemies are code officials eyeing long-delayed violations, neighbors suspicious of gentrification, community activists who fear displacement, and sellers nursing wounded pride. Expect hostility; prepare charm offensives and ironclad plans.

Conquest also demands speed. The building is bleeding every day you wait to close roofs leaks, utilities run, opportunity cost accrues. Yet recklessness invites ruin. Thus the conqueror is paradox: audacious but meticulous, lightning-fast but data-driven.

3. The Due-Diligence Playbook for Distressed and Value-Add Deals

A. Situational Intelligence
Before touring, assemble a dossier: mortgage details from county recorders, code-violation histories, litigation dockets, UCC filings on everything from laundry machines to chillers. Identify whether you must negotiate with owners, receivers, servicers, or bankruptcy trustees. Each has distinct motivations and approval timelines.

B. Deal-Stage Environmental Recon
For heavy distress, order a Phase I environmental site assessment immediately and include a Phase II trigger if any

recognized environmental condition surfaces. Gas spills, dry-cleaning solvents, or buried heating-oil tanks can transform a heroic rescue into a tripwire of unlimited cleanup liability. Machiavelli speaks of fortifying captured cities; in modern deals, fortification begins with soil samples.

C. Capital-Expenditure Mapping

Walk units without power; feel drywall dampness; photograph boiler serial numbers. Build a line-item budget for cure costs and desirability upgrades: envelope remediation, window replacements, amenity additions. Add a contingency not below twenty percent. During conquest you will unearth problems too late for renegotiation; your contingency is the loyal cohort ready to die beside you.

D. Rent-Roll Forensics

Distressed properties often show collections, not accruals. Insist on bank-statement verification for each month of the past year, segregated by unit. Match tenant names against court-eviction portals; the current owner may call delinquencies "payment plans." Where occupancy sits below breakeven, underwrite to a lease-up schedule that factors concession burn-off and marketing spend.

E. Community and Political Stakeholders

Meet the alderman, the zoning commissioner, and neighborhood association presidents *before* closing. Present a high-level improvement plan and ask for feedback. Document every handshake promise. When Machiavelli writes that "people should either be caressed or crushed," he is blunt about stakes: win allies early, or prepare for open warfare.

F. Financing Architecture

Traditional lenders flee messy titles and negative NOI. Court private credit funds, hedge funds, or family-office mezzanine willing to bankroll the value-add path. Structure draws tied to milestones—roof dried-in, plumbing rough-ins complete—to keep investors comfortable. Negotiate interest reserves within the loan so debt service does not sabotage construction cash flow.

G. Execution Timeline
Draft a Gantt chart that starts with permit submission on day one after closing. Parallel-process everything—order materials while architects finish stamped plans, pre-hire subcontractors pending successful title transfer. Delays are interest-burning bonfires. Your timeline is the siege ladder; if its rungs break, the wall stands unscaled.

H. Exit Viability Check
Underwrite your exit multiple ways: stabilized refinance, condo map, portfolio roll-up for REIT sale. If none pencil above an acceptable IRR even using conservative cap rates, the conquest is foolhardy. Victory without harvest is defeat in disguise.

Part III – Weighing the Paths and Switching Playbooks

1. Cycle-Sensitive Strategy

Inheritance excels late in the expansion when prices peak but liquidity flows freely; banks clamor for low-risk loans and equity expects gentle yields. Conquest shines in downturns or early recovery when distress surfaces and competition retreats. Learning both arts means you can pivot as seasons change, hunting where prey is abundant rather than forcing tactics onto unyielding terrain.

2. Personal Temperament and Team Composition

An operator who loathes construction chaos should favor hereditary states, perhaps layering in mild value-add. A founder who thrives on turning rubble into lofts will suffocate running stabilized suburban offices. Evaluate not only your taste but your bench: Can your asset manager recalibrate from Class B suburban infill to urban adaptive reuse? Are your lenders equally comfortable across risk spectra? Align ambitions with capacity or build new capacity before crossing genre lines.

3. Hybrid Opportunities

Occasionally a stabilized asset hides a conquest option—a zoning overlay that allows an extra floor, a cell-tower lease ready to sign, an under-market parking garage begging for dynamic pricing. Conversely, a distressed building can carry an inheritable component: perhaps the ground floor is leased long-term to a medical group, providing bond-like income that underwrites the rehab of the vacant upper stories. The shrewd investor slices the deal, financing each layer with capital matching its risk while managing the whole under one coordinated command.

Part IV – Common Pitfalls and Antidotes

1. Over-Paying for Peace

Hereditary assets lure buyers into low-cap-rate bidding wars. Remember Machiavelli's warning: "Men more quickly forget the death of their father than the loss of their patrimony." Your investors will forgive dusty corridors sooner than they forgive a dividend cut. If projected cash-on-cash shrinks below your hurdle because competition is insane, withdraw and wait. You cannot recoup basis in a flat-rent future.

2. Under-Estimating the Cost of War

In conquests, optimism kills. Accept that every distressed project hides at least one latent catastrophe—structural beam rot, unpermitted electrical, asbestos in mastic. Double contingencies for assets older than 1978 and triple them if built before 1940.

3. Culture Clash After Takeover

Staff accustomed to mom-and-pop informality may revolt when introduced to institutional reporting lines; valuable employees walk, leaving you short-handed mid-renovation. Stage listening sessions, roll out new SOPs in phases, and tie bonuses to measurable improvements. Machiavelli notes that "the nature of peoples is fickle"; guide that fickleness toward productivity before someone else channels it toward sabotage.

Part V – The Integrated Decision Matrix

Before issuing a letter of intent, answer six questions:

1. **Market Position** – Does local absorption favor swift lease-up or justify paying premium for stability?

2. **Capital Availability** – Do your investors crave current yield or patient upside?

3. **Operational Bandwidth** – Can your team execute a heavy lift while managing existing assets?

4. **Regulatory Climate** – Is city hall pro-development or eyeing rent caps?

5. **Portfolio Balance** – Will this acquisition diversify risk or stack exposure in one segment?

6. **Personal Edge** – Do you hold an unfair advantage here—relationship, expertise, data insight?

A yes to questions one through three in the direction of stability points to inheritance; yes in the direction of upside and you saddle for conquest. A mismatch signals delay or partnership with specialists who supply missing pieces.

Epilogue: The Prince at the Fork

Machiavelli closes one chapter by reminding rulers that fortune "is the arbiter of half our actions." The other half rests on choice. Whether you inherit a purring income machine or storm the barricades of a derelict mill, mastery lies in matching action to context. Study the craft until the smell of fresh asphalt or peeling paint tells you instantly which playbook to open. Then commit without half-measures, for "fortune is a woman," and she yields to the decisive. Whether your flag rises calmly over a peaceful duchy or snaps in gritty wind above a raw redoubt, you will know it as yours—won by judgment, guarded by diligence, and destined, through vigilance, to endure.

Chapter 4 – Winning Without War: Negotiation Tactics

Opening Note: The Silent Battlefield

Machiavelli understood that power often shifts before blades cross. "The wise man," he observed, "does at once what the fool does finally." In real-estate negotiations, that wisdom shows up as a contract signed, a handshake sealed, long before rivals even realize the game has begun. This chapter dissects how to win the asset while everyone else is still sharpening pencils: by controlling information, calibrating emotion, and composing offers so compelling that acceptance feels inevitable—yet always at a price that preserves your upside.

Part I – Leveraging Information Asymmetry

1. Why Knowledge Is the Only Legal Cheat Code

Markets preach transparency, but every deal hides wrinkles: an undisclosed easement, a key tenant on the verge of bankruptcy, a grandfathered zoning clause worth millions. Whoever spots these first shapes the entire math of the transaction. Machiavelli wrote, "He who knows how to deceive will always find someone who will allow himself to be deceived." In our century the word *deceive* is radioactive; replace it with *discover*, and the principle remains.

Discovery lets you tilt the board without lying—simply by seeing what the other side missed.

2. Building the Intelligence Lattice

Micro-data scrape. Install a standing alert that pulls every building permit, code violation, and eviction filing within three miles of your target property. A sudden cluster of plumbing permits tells you pipes are collapsing city-wide—valuable leverage when you ask for a price adjustment.

Ground whispers. Walk the neighborhood and talk to convenience-store clerks, delivery drivers, postal workers. They witness patterns no spreadsheet shows: nightly loitering, new company shuttles, emerging commuter shortcuts. One off-duty patrol officer mentioning a planned police substation can let you underwrite lower future crime risk before brokers bake that into comps.

Deep lease archaeology. Read every line of major tenant leases going back two generations. You may find an obscure option clause that forces rent to reset upward with CPI plus a sweetheart kicker the current owner never enforced. Promptly calculate the forward revenue pop, then decide whether to reveal it—or to keep quiet and pay the seller's asking price on their stale assumptions.

Seller psychology scan. Information asymmetry isn't just hard data; it's motive. Is the seller over-levered? Mid-divorce? Nearing a loan maturity they can't refinance? Once you know *why* they must sell, you design deal terms that soothe that specific pain while costing you little. Offer a twenty-day close with no financing contingency to a seller drowning in extension fees; watch them drop price by seven figures in gratitude.

3. Using Silence and Sequencing

Control flow. Never reveal your underwriting spreadsheet before you have squeezed every drop of intel from the other side. Ask broad questions early—occupancy history, cap-ex—but reveal almost nothing about your thresholds. Once their story is set, you tighten the net with granular follow-ups whose answers you likely already know from third-party sleuthing. Inconsistencies emerge. The gap between their answers and your data becomes leverage for concessions—without an ounce of bluffing.

4. Ethical Edges Only

Machiavelli advised that appearances matter as much as deeds. Exploiting information asymmetry must stay on the sunny side of legality and reputation. You are not misrepresenting facts; you are **authoring the narrative** by choosing which facts to highlight, which to hold, and which to monetize after closing. "It is not titles that honor men," he noted, "but men that honor titles." Your name is the title that gets you first looks at future deals; guard it by wielding knowledge, not deception.

Part II – Fear vs. Love at the Bargaining Table

1. The Eternal Dilemma

"Upon this a question arises," Machiavelli wrote, "whether it be better to be loved than feared or feared than loved." In negotiations the answer is: both, but at different moments and aimed at different actors. Your counterpart must love the *outcome* you are offering yet fear the *alternatives* they face if they stall.

2. Engineering Respectful Fear

Timelines as weapons. Draft your letter of intent with an expiration inside forty-eight hours. Signal that capital is mobile and discipline ruthless. The ticking clock triggers loss aversion: they fear missing the only sure buyer in a softening market.

Proof of capacity. Attach redacted bank statements or an endorsement letter from your lender confirming funds are committed. Fear emerges organically: the seller realizes delay might hand the prize to someone with less certainty, more haggling.

Credible walk-away posture. Never bluster. Instead, prepare a parallel opportunity so if the negotiation turns theatrical you can exit calmly, citing capital re-allocation. True fear dawns when the opposite chair senses they cannot overplay greed without losing you for good.

3. Manufacturing Earned Love

Solve their headache first. If the seller's real problem is an impending balloon payment, open by offering a release of earnest money at contract signing to cover it. They will associate your presence with immediate relief—an emotion closer to love than mere liking.

Honor their legacy. Owners who built the asset from dirt often care who stewards it next. Share your renovation vision, preservation plans, or philanthropic tie-ins to the neighborhood. Respect fills the emotional bank; when final numbers tighten, they forgive a low-ball more than they would from a spreadsheet-flipping stranger.

Transparency milestones. After each diligence phase, provide a brief memo summarizing what you learned, what remains, and any concerns. This openness breeds trust that you are not angling for a last-minute re-trade without cause. People favor deals that feel just.

4. Balancing Act and Non-verbal Signals

You cannot recite Machiavelli across the conference table, but you can embody his dual approach. Sit upright, speak slowly, keep voice level—project calm competence. Smile genuinely when granting a concession, pause and lean back when rejecting one. The shift from warmth to firmness and back reminds the other side that you govern wide emotional bandwidths. Love feels near; fear lurks in the wings.

5. Managing Third-Party Perceptions

Brokers, attorneys, and lenders watch your conduct. If they sense ruthless fairness—tough on price, impeccable on performance—they ferry that reputation elsewhere. Future sellers enter talks already half-inclined to trust your process because intermediaries vouched for your integrity. As Machiavelli says, "The first method for estimating the intelligence of a ruler is to look at the men he has around him." Fill the room with professionals who testify, by their presence, to your closing prowess.

Part III – Crafting Irresistible Offers Without Overpaying

1. Reframing Value Away from Price

Everyone proclaims "highest and best," yet many sellers crave *surest and soonest*. Package certainty, speed, and ego-honor so attractively that headline price fades in importance. Your task: strip away elements that cost you little but feel precious to them, layering those onto a firm but disciplined number.

2. The Term-Sheet Toolkit

Hard earnest money with an escape hatch. Offer six-figure non-refundable deposit day one, but escrow an equal sum held back from closing adjustments. If due diligence unearths hidden defects, that escrow offsets the repair credit. The seller sees fearless commitment; you see built-in insurance.

Reverse 1031 accommodation. If the seller plans a like-kind exchange but lacks an upleg, volunteer your qualified intermediary to facilitate a *reverse* structure, giving them extra weeks. Administrative headache to you, existential tax question solved for them. In return, shave basis off the price.

Post-closing cooperation covenant. Promise to provide limited financial reporting for a year so the seller's accountants can finalize returns. Cost to you: a junior analyst's time. Perceived value to them: fewer IRS nightmares.

Seller carry-back at junior lien. When financing gets choppy, propose that the seller hold a small second mortgage. Offer interest above senior debt but below mezz markets. They earn incremental yield, you lower blended rate and lighten equity check—enough savings to justify meeting their price ceiling.

3. Option-Suite Offers

Present two versions of your purchase:

1. **The Lightning Close.** Lower price, hard deposit, fifteen-day due diligence, cash wiring inside thirty days. Appeals to sellers craving liquidity.

2. **The Legacy Plan.** Slightly higher price, ninety-day closing, joint press release praising the seller's community impact, option for them to retain minority equity. Appeals to owners who want status more than liquidation.

By framing choices, you anchor negotiation around *which* version, not *if* they will sell. Make both models profitable; let them choose ego-fit.

4. Cost Discipline Through Reverse Engineering

Set your walk-away cap rate or yield first. Reverse-engineer maximum price, embed buffer for unexpected capital outlays, and freeze that ceiling. Every sweetener you add must be funded by trimming elsewhere—usually timeline concessions or creative financing. The moment concessions push the all-in cost above your ceiling, politely withdraw. Machiavelli's hard lesson: "A prince who is himself not wise cannot be well advised." Your spreadsheet is the silent advisor that arrests emotional overreach.

5. Negotiating Credits Instead of Discounts

Some sellers choke on visible price cuts because appraisals, partner optics, or loan covenants reference face value. Offer full ask but demand closing credits for roof replacement, HVAC end-of-life, or outstanding taxes. You preserve IRR, they preserve bragging rights. Credits can be financed when price is not—increasing leverage against those same repairs you would have funded with cash.

6. Timing the Offer Strike

Monitor interest-rate announcements, fiscal quarter endings, and holidays. Drop offers when competing bidders are distracted—mid-December, late Friday afternoons, or the week the Federal Reserve meets. Sellers tired of uncertainty after long marketing campaigns often capitulate to a strong, simple term sheet just as fatigue peaks. Patience is silent capital.

7. Deadlocks and the Power of Small Gives

When talks stall, introduce a minor concession with symbolic heft: let the seller keep a historic neon sign they adore, or agree to rename a courtyard after the founder. Such gestures cost almost nothing yet unlock reciprocity. As Machiavelli put it, "Men are won over by the same means—from whatever rank they are."

8. Post-Acceptance Vigilance

Winning an LOI is only half the war; now guard against *price creep* in the opposite direction. Vendors may inflate quotes, inspectors can over-specify repairs, lenders might add covenants. Maintain your original return model as tablets of stone. Any new dollar must be offset by a credit or renegotiated term or it slips directly from investor pocket to project bloat. Command discipline meetings weekly; kill scope drift early. Victory, as Machiavelli warned, often "dissolves in weakness" once conquering armies grow lazy.

Conclusion: The Art of Seamless Triumph

Negotiation in real estate is neither a duel nor a peace treaty. It is an intricate dance where you lead invisibly, guiding partners to the exact spot you marked on the floor before the music started. You see angles early through information asymmetry, temper the room's emotions by choreographing fear and love, and weave offer terms that feel like velvet though they are stitched with iron mathematical thread. Machiavelli closes *The Prince* urging leaders to act decisively, to "seize the initiative" rather than wait for fortune's favor. Steel yourself with data, wrap it in empathy, press forward with unwavering cost discipline, and you will take territories without firing a shot—your wealth compounding quietly while louder men clash swords in the courtyard, wondering how you already own the castle.

Chapter 5 – Dealing with Tenants and Sellers as Subjects

Prelude: The Crown and the Crowd

Machiavelli never uses the word "tenant," yet his pages drip with advice on governing people who do not share your bloodline or your ambitions. "A prince must lay firm foundations," he writes, "otherwise he will inevitably be ruined." In real-estate ownership, those foundations are the rules that bind landlord and occupant, buyer and seller, long before trouble shows its teeth. Treat every tenant and every seller as a subject who can support—or sabotage—your reign. The art is to rule firmly enough that rebellion is futile, yet generously enough that rebellion is unnecessary.

Part I – Establishing Early Authority: Clear Leases, Firm Policies

1. First Impressions Carve Hierarchies

Machiavelli warns that "he who is the cause of another becoming powerful is ruined," because dependency flips the power dynamic. When you allow a tenant to dictate lease terms or define maintenance standards, you grant them authority that should reside only with you. The lease—signed before keys change hands—is the founding constitution of your micro-state. Draft it with the precision of a treaty and the foresight of a battle plan.

- **Precision over prettiness.** A plain-language lease, 12-point font, no Latin phrases. Complexity breeds loopholes, and loopholes breed power shifts.

- **Time-boxed rent grace.** Five days, not ten. Automatic late fees on day six. Machiavelli's maxim applies: "It is better to be impetuous than cautious." Swift enforcement shows you mean every syllable.

- **Repair protocol hierarchy.** Emergencies phone-in; routine fixes through an online portal; unauthorized repairs forbidden. Clear funnel prevents tenants from staging a "maintenance mutiny": organizing receipts and demanding reimbursements outside your system.

- **Renewal and rent-increase clauses.** Spell out the index (CPI + 2% or market rent survey) and timeline. Ambiguity invites debate; debate metastasizes into grievance.

2. Onboarding as Coronation

Tenants decide within the first week whether you are sovereign or supplicant. Conduct a five-point "welcome audit":

1. **Key handover ceremony.** In-person or via a branded lockbox. Explain parking, trash, emergency numbers. They must see you—or your manager—as accessible monarch,

not absent overlord.

2. **Orientation email within 24 hours.** Summarize lease highlights in bullet form, attach PDF. Repetition imprints rule of law.

3. **Maintenance phone test.** Call your own emergency line at 2 am before tenants ever need it. If you can't reach a live agent, you forfeited authority before the first toilet overflows.

4. **Proactive inspection schedule.** Annual or semiannual walk-through announced at move-in. The rule exists before problems emerge, so no one can later cry harassment.

5. **Autopay enrollment push.** Offer a one-time $25 credit for signing up. You shift payment reliability from human willpower to algorithmic certainty.

3. Seller Counterparties: Authority in the Transaction Room

When buying off-market property from long-time owners, the power dynamic can wobble. Sellers may feel parental rights over the asset, you the presumptive heir. Reset roles early:

- **Define single point of contact.** Multiparty families breed cross-talk. Require a designated representative. You negotiate with one voice, avoiding "good cop, bad cop" oscillations.

- **Set document deadlines.** Data room populated within seven days or LOI voids. You become timekeeper; they chase you, not vice versa.

- **Insist on estoppels and lien releases upfront.** This signals you control closing mechanics. Machiavelli's counsel—"injuries should be inflicted all at once"—translates: impose strict requirements early, before goodwill accumulates.

Part II – Balancing Firmness and Goodwill

1. The Dual Currency of Rule

Machiavelli's most-quoted balance beam—"It is much safer to be feared than loved, if one has to lack one of the two"—contains a hidden fuse: "A prince must nevertheless make himself feared in such a manner that, if he does not gain love, he avoids hatred." In rental operations, hatred germinates lawsuits and rent strikes. Fear with fairness keeps the peace.

2. Structural Fairness

- **Transparent ledgers.** Tenants may request proof of utility pass-throughs. Publish an anonymized cost breakdown once a year: total water bill, total billed back, methodology. Mystery breeds conspiracy; transparency defuses it.

- **Maintenance SLA scoreboard.** Post average response times in the lobby bulletin or resident portal. Pride drives your team to meet targets; residents trust numbers over promises.

- **Responsive escalation tree.** Tier 1: onsite manager replies within four business hours. Tier 2: regional manager within 24. Tier 3: ownership email inside 48. Publicizing the route to the top reduces social-media venting.

3. Gestures of Generosity that Cost Little

- **Lease-anniversary thank-you.** A $10 coffee card and a note: "You've called 123 Main home for two years—thank you for staying." Ten-second gesture buys reservoir of goodwill for the next 3% rent bump.

- **Community microgrants.** Allocate $2,500 yearly for resident-proposed projects: garden plots, library boxes, mural walls. Funded by operations, marketed as gift. Tenants own the improvement, literally and emotionally.

- **Grace in catastrophe.** A single, well-timed rent deferment during a verified medical crisis echoes for years. Machiavelli advises occasional largesse: "A prince ought to show himself a lover of virtue... giving rewards to men of merit." Modern translation: help good payers through unavoidable storms, but document terms tightly.

4. Non-Negotiables

Fairness is not softness. The following are immutable:

- Past-due rent triggers late fee automatically.

- Unauthorized occupants void lease.

- Pets follow breed/weight rules or face immediate notice.

Carve exceptions only via written addenda with compensating consideration (higher deposit, accelerated rent increase, shorter renewal term). Exceptions without compensation are seeds of inequality, and inequality decays into anger.

5. Seller Relations: Honoring Legacy While Protecting Capital

Offer sellers post-closing updates—a quarterly email with occupancy and renovation photos—especially if they still live nearby. This courtesy costs minutes, defuses seller's remorse, and fosters future referrals. Yet maintain boundary: no decision veto rights. Their era ended at closing.

Part III – Case Studies Where Leniency Bred Revolt

Case Study 1: The Three-Month Waiver That Spawned a Year-Long Rent Strike

Background

 A mid-Atlantic owner inherited a 64-unit building with 40% Section 8 tenants. During a boiler failure in January, management waived February rent for all residents as apology. Repairs finished in two weeks, but the waiver stood.

Leniency Spiral

 March invoices listed full rent again. Several tenants, citing precedent, withheld payment, claiming "the owners promised a free month whenever heat fails." Word spread on social media; a tenant union formed. By May, 28 units were participating in a coordinated strike.

Revolt Mechanics

- The waiver lacked documentation linking it to a one-time event.

- Management failed to hold listening sessions after resumption, allowing rumors.

- Late-fee notices arrived en masse, perceived as retaliation.

Outcome

 After six months and $180,000 unpaid rent, owner negotiated a settlement forgiving half balances and funding HVAC upgrades. Legal fees topped $45,000. Machiavelli's verdict: clemency without foresight invites contempt. A targeted credit only for units below 65°F, plus memorandum signed by each tenant, could have expressed goodwill without eroding authority.

Case Study 2: The Eviction Compassion That Encouraged Serial Abuse

Background
 In a Sunbelt duplex portfolio, an owner prided himself on "second-chance housing." A tenant who fell 45 days behind due to job loss promised catch-up within two pay cycles. Owner ignored the lease's 10-day pay-or-quit clause and accepted a handshake.

Leniency Ripples
 Tenant caught up after 60 days, celebrated on neighborhood Facebook group. Over the next year five other tenants requested similar grace. Delinquencies crushed cash flow; the lender flagged DSCR covenant breach.

Revolt Phase
 When the owner finally issued strict notices, tenants labeled him a hypocrite. The local paper ran a sympathetic piece on "landlord reversals," amplifying reputational damage. Machiavelli: "Benefits should be conferred gradually; and in that way they will taste better." Early over-generosity raised expectations; later enforcement felt like betrayal.

Case Study 3: Seller Carry-Back Gone Rogue

Background
 An aging motel owner agreed to carry 20% seller financing for a value-add buyer, interest-only for two years. Covenants required monthly performance updates. Six months in, the buyer missed

two update deadlines while juggling renovations; the seller grew anxious.

Leniency Misstep
To avoid tension, buyer's rep told seller "updates optional until year end." Feeling ignored, the seller hired counsel to accelerate note repayment, citing technical default. Legal escrow froze renovation funds, delaying project.

Outcome
Buyer paid steep attorney fees and a $35k note-modification surcharge. A simple, scheduled Zoom call series would have preserved the relationship. Machiavelli: "Men are ungrateful, fickle, false… while you work for their benefit they are entirely yours; they offer you their blood, property, life. But… they change." Anticipate change by codifying every concession.

Part IV – Protocols for Crisis Response

1. The "Two-Hour Window" Rule

When a revolt flickers—late rent swell, public complaint—respond within two hours. Not solve, simply acknowledge: "We're investigating, expect full reply tomorrow." Silence hardens suspicion.

2. Triangulate Facts Fast

Pull lease, payment ledger, maintenance tickets. Interview onsite staff and, when safe, tenant reps. Compile a timeline. Machiavelli prepared dossiers on conspirators before acting; you map facts before confronting.

3. Offer Narrow Solutions

Address the core grievance only. Volunteer too many fixes and you reveal desperation. Example: "Assuming inspection confirms the leak, we will credit the water damage portion of your July rent as allowed under Section 12." Specific, contractual, finite.

4. Escalate Decisively

If peaceful remedies fail, file eviction or lawsuit swiftly. Public show of resolve deters imitators. Yet pair action with respectful messaging: "We value every resident, but timely rent is essential to maintain services." Fear without hatred.

Part V – Institutionalizing Balanced Rulership

1. Policy Handbook as Shield

Publish a resident handbook distilling lease obligations into Q&A. Include emergency numbers, payment portals, noise rules, pet policies, inspection calendar. A shared text becomes arbiter; debates end with a page reference, not a shouting match.

2. Ongoing Consent Culture

Collect digital sign-offs each time you update amenity rules or parking decals. Tenants click "I agree," reinforcing contractual tie.

Machiavelli loved public ceremonies swearing loyalty; digital equivalents keep modern subjects aligned.

3. Staff Training in Micro-Authority

Train maintenance techs to cite policy kindly but firmly: "I'm happy to fix this outlet, Ms. Davis, but per page 7 I need a work order in the system first." Every employee becomes an ambassador of the principality's laws.

4. Annual Policy Review

Laws ossify. Gather rent-roll data, delinquency stats, violation logs, and evaluate whether policies remain fair and enforceable. Amend in offseason when turnover low. Communicate changes 60 days in advance.

Epilogue: Governance That Endures

Machiavelli concludes that a prince's greatest defense is "not to be hated by the people." For real-estate rulers, that hinges on predictable justice: clear leases enforced consistently, kindness deployed strategically, and mercy granted with documentation and sunset clauses. Tenants and sellers become loyal subjects not because you smile but because you keep chaos at bay—and because, when you do flex generosity, it feels deliberate, precious, and rare.

Govern long enough under these principles and word spreads: this landlord plays hardball on the rules yet never cheats; this buyer closes fast and honors promises. In an industry where reputation circulates faster than press releases, that balanced renown is the moat around your empire. Rivals may copy your spreadsheets, but they cannot counterfeit years of disciplined fairness. And when storms—economic, political, or viral—sweep through the realm, the subjects who believe in your leadership will tighten their belts, pay the rent, sign the addendum, or extend the carry-back, knowing your firm hand has guided them through worse.

Thus the modern prince secures his state not with armies but with PDFs, not with edicts but with calendars, not with terror but with the unflinching promise that order will prevail—and that those who keep the covenant will share in the prosperity of the realm.

Chapter 6 – Fortresses, Moats, and Maintenance

Preface: The Walls That Matter

When Machiavelli warned that "a prince who has not got his own forces will be ruined," he meant more than armies. He meant defenses—structures that hold when fortune turns hostile. In property investing, those defenses span bricks, bylaws, and bandwidth. A roof that sheds rain, a covenant that blocks a rival's liquor store, a camera that texts you when a boiler room door opens at 2 a.m.—each is a stone in the fortress or a trench in the moat. This chapter unpacks how to build and maintain all three layers so that storms, lawsuits, and thieves break themselves against your perimeter.

Part I – Physical Fortresses: Inspections and Preventive Repairs

1. The Castle Analogy Still Stands

Castles outlived sieges because their keep, curtain walls, and barbicans each served as sacrificial barriers. In real estate, load-bearing masonry, waterproof membranes, and mechanical cores mirror that hierarchy. Lose the outer layer—tar flashings fail—and you still have redundant drains. But if the inner keep—your structural frame—crumbles, the realm collapses. Machiavelli hammered this truth when he said a prince must "place in safety those towns which might offer opposition" and "strengthen the weakest points." Translate: identify failure nodes and reinforce them before opponents—weather, wear, vandals—exploit gaps.

2. The Four-Season Inspection Cycle

Spring – Envelope and Grounds.
 Walk the roof immediately after the first thaw. Look for popped nails, blistered membrane, clogged scuppers. Inspect grading; winter frost-heave can tilt sidewalks toward foundations. Catching a quarter-inch slope reversal now costs a landscaping crew one afternoon; ignoring it means spalling brick and moldy drywall next year.

Summer – Mechanical and Fire Safety.
 Warm weather lets boilers be shut down for deep clean and ultrasonic thickness testing. Diesel generators run shorter loads when ambient air is hot, revealing coolant or oil leaks in real conditions. Fire panels receive dust-off and device address testing. Machiavelli's dictum—"It is much safer to anticipate than to wait"—echoes in every gasket swapped during downtime.

Autumn – Thermal Envelope and Gutters.
 As leaves fall, clear downspouts weekly, not once. End-of-season gutter debris is the number-one cause of ice dams that shear shingles and soak insulation. Infrared thermography scans walls at dusk when interior heat meets evening chill, revealing missing

batts or compromised spray foam. Repair before the first freeze locks damage in place.

Winter – Interior and Life-Safety Drills.
 Snow drifts expose heat-loss patterns on roofs; uneven melt indicates insulation gaps. Conduct unannounced fire-door releases and carbon-monoxide alarm tests. Record tenant response times and adjust evacuation maps. A castle's garrison drilled constantly; your tenants become unofficial sentries when they know exits and alarms by heart.

3. Predictive Maintenance Metrics

Move from calendar-driven upkeep to data-driven prediction:

Vibration analysis on rooftop units flags bearing failure months ahead.
 Oil sampling in elevators detects bronze wear debris early enough to replace thrust bearings during scheduled lulls.
 Runtime counters on sump pumps trigger service at 10,000-cycle increments instead of arbitrary dates.

Each sensorized insight echoes Machiavelli's praise for princes who "recognize misfortunes at a distance." He compared them to physicians sensing disease before it festers. Your IoT dashboards are that stethoscope.

4. Capital Reserve Strategy

Reserve studies must assume worst-case lead times. Ordering a 500-ton chiller today can take 36 weeks; wait until it dies and your tenants simmer. Fund capital accounts at a rate that covers 130 percent of projected five-year replacements because supply-chain shocks love to shred budgets. When critics whisper you over-reserve, quote the Florentine: "Men sooner forget the death of their father than the loss of their patrimony." Capital reserves protect patrimony—yours and theirs.

5. Staff Culture: The Knightly Code

Castles fell when guards slept. Require maintenance techs to photo-document each inspection detail in a cloud log. Reward the technician who finds the hairline crack others missed. Rotate night-shift patrols so complacency never breeds blind spots. "A prince ought to inspire fear in such a way that, if he has not love, he may at least not have hatred." In facilities, fear of skipping a checklist should outweigh laziness, yet respect for leadership's fairness keeps morale high.

Part II – Legal Moats: Zoning, Covenants, Insurance

1. The Invisible Trenches

Physical walls halt swords; paperwork stops attorneys and code-enforcement officers. Machiavelli advised founding new principalities with laws tailored to secure power. Your counterpart is a sheath of documents that channel threats away from the balance sheet.

2. Zoning Armor

Spot-Upzoning as Blade and Shield
 Secure entitlements that allow denser or mixed use than neighbors. That bonus floor area becomes both profit engine and deterrent: competitors know city council won't re-grant such favors easily, so they shop elsewhere. Maintain good-neighbor policies—lighting cutoffs, traffic studies—to pre-empt opposition. The prince who conquers and then "injures all his enemies at once" echoes here: face community concerns in a single, proactive session, mitigate sincerely, then build under protection of settled law.

Overlay District Surveillance
 Cities slide new overlays—historic, signage, floodplain—like thieves in the night. Monitor planning-board agendas monthly. Early notice lets you lobby, adapt designs, or—if coming rules strangle value—sell before buyers read the minutes.

3. Covenants and Easements

Restrictive Covenants
 Record use limits that benefit you: prohibit drive-throughs on pad sites if you own the adjacent sit-down restaurant; ban rooftop billboards that would overshadow your signage. Covenants outlive individual ownership; they are Machiavelli's permanent garrisons.

Access Easements
 Grant or acquire driveway easements with mutual maintenance language. Clarity today averts litigation tomorrow. Where easements are one-sided, collect a fee or higher rent because you are conferring perpetual advantage. This is taxation without resentment, extracted at sale closing rather than via annual confrontations.

4. Insurance as Standing Army

Property and Casualty
 Specify full-replacement cost endorsements, not depreciated actual-cash-value. Add ordinance-or-law coverage for 100 percent rebuild to current code; old buildings are like medieval towns—grandfathered until burnt, then subject to modern rules.

Environmental Liability
 Phase-I clean bills lose value if underground tanks later leak. Pollution-legal-liability policies bridge that gap. High deductibles offset seldom claims; treat premiums as shield rent.

Builder's Risk
 During renovations, a half-completed wing is more flammable than finished units. Confirm policy permits partial occupancy and covers soft-cost overruns. Machiavelli urged princes to arm even during peace; builder's-risk is the sword over the hearth.

Cyber and Ransomware
 Smart locks and payment portals expose you to hackers. Policy riders for social-engineering fraud and data restoration mitigate ransom risk. Failure to insure digital trenches is the modern equivalent of leaving the postern gate unlocked.

5. Legal Audit Cadence

Schedule an annual "moat review" with counsel: validate that certificates list correct entities, confirm additional insured endorsements for vendors, test disaster-recovery clauses. Amendments keep pace with asset changes—new playgrounds, solar arrays, food trucks. Each adjustment thickens the moat.

Part III – Tech Moats: Smart-Home Monitoring and Security Systems

1. From Drawbridge to Dashboard

A medieval portcullis fell at the pull of a chain; today, a smartphone app locks 300 doors at once. Technology expands control radius while shrinking response time. Yet each sensor is a spy that can betray you if unsecured. Build systems as layered as physical walls, then encrypt them like diplomatic pouches.

2. Core Components of the Tech Fortress

Access Control
 Cloud-managed locks with individual codes end key-copy vulnerabilities. Time-bound credentials for vendors vanish at midnight. Audit trails log every latch event. Tenants feel safety; you feel oversight.

Environmental Sensors
 LoRaWAN or NB-IoT water sensors in every wet wall ping leaks before tenants smell mildew. Temperature probes in attics alert against HVAC failure during heat waves. Data funnels into a single pane of glass—your war room.

Surveillance Intelligence
 Cameras running edge-analytics detect humans loitering beyond five minutes. The system texts guards a clip, not hours of footage. Privacy laws differ by state; post signage and mask

apartment-windows zones to avoid claims. Remember Machiavelli's tactic of watching foes without them sensing spies; transparency signage reconciles modern ethics with vigilance.

Energy Optimization
Smart thermostats tied to vacancy sensors shave peak loads. Utility APIs feed dashboards that compare usage across sister properties, highlighting anomalies. Reduced kilowatt spend funds reserve accounts—turning data into literal fortress stones.

3. Cybersecurity Layers

Zero-Trust Networks
Isolate building systems from tenant Wi-Fi. Even within operations, segment HVAC from access-control VLANs. If one falls, others stand, like concentric castle yards.

Credential Hygiene
Rotate admin passwords quarterly. Employ multi-factor authentication. Lax creds at a Vegas hotel let hackers jump from aquarium sensor to high-roller database; do not replicate that farce.

Firmware Vigilance
Schedule midnight auto-updates with rollback plan. Run vulnerability scans monthly. Machiavelli warned against mercenaries who switch sides; unpatched firmware is a mercenary waiting to be bribed.

4. Data Ownership and Monetization

Collect usage stats ethically and monetize them responsibly:

Aggregate Water Data lets you negotiate bulk-rate savings with utilities.
 Foot-Traffic Analytics from common-area cameras displays heat maps you can sell to pop-up retailers.

Offer tenants opt-in perks: lower rent for sharing thermostat data. Framed as partnership, not extraction, this mirrors Machiavelli's insight: "A wise prince… will contrive that things depend on him." Tenants who benefit from your platform cling to it.

5. Emergency Integration

Marry tech moat to first-responder protocols:

Mass-Notification Buttons broadcast voice and SMS alerts building-wide.
 Fire-panel API Bridges unlock stairwells automatically for trucks.
 Mechanical Shutdown Scripts kill gas lines during earthquake sensor triggers.

These automations cut decision lag when chaos erupts—fulfilling Machiavelli's command that rulers act "swiftly and decisively."

6. Tech Depreciation Schedules

Hardware obsolescence is the enemy inside the gate. Budget replacement at 50 percent of manufacturer-promised life; hedge with modular systems that accept new firmware and swappable boards. Five-year capital forecasts should list IoT devices alongside boilers.

Integration: The Fortress Mentality in Daily Operations

1. Cross-Domain Incident Tabletop Drills

Quarterly, run mixed-scenario drills: pipe bursts (physical), triggers insurance claim (legal), leaks footage online (tech). Debrief to refine SOPs. Cross-training staff prevents silo blind spots.

2. KPI Dashboard—Your Watchtower

Combine work-order age, reserve balance, insurance expirations, and sensor alerts into a single dashboard visible to asset managers daily. Spikes demand immediate council—mirroring the medieval watchtower whose bell summoned archers.

3. Budget Alignment

Allocate OPEX 3 percent of gross income to routine fortress care, CAPEX 15 percent of effective rent to long-term masonry. Protect these lines from acquisition-driven cost shaving; selling the moat to buy extra archers—marketing, amenities—leaves the keep naked.

Closing Reflections: The Price of Impregnability

Machiavelli's Italy teemed with minor lords who built splendid keeps yet fell to bribery, neglect, or plague. Your modern principality can crumble if you undervalue any moat layer. A pristine roof won't stop a judgment if an ADA ramp is missing; perfect covenants won't deter hackers siphoning rent payments.

Resilience grows from redundancy, vigilance, and adaptation. Schedule walks on parapets—roof hatches and server logs alike. Audit the moat—legal binders and firmware. Fortify the keep—foundation piles and capital reserves. And when outsiders marvel that your empire stands unshaken while theirs flood, crack, or burn, you will recall the Florentine's wisdom: "Whosoever desires constant success must change his conduct with the times." The fortress is never finished; it is a verb you practice—inspect, insure, encrypt—until the walls extend beyond masonry into mindset, a culture steel-rimmed against entropy.

Chapter 7 – The Right Hand of the Prince: Property Managers

Prelude: Why the Prince Cannot Rule Alone

Machiavelli judged a ruler's caliber by the company he kept. "The first method for estimating the intelligence of a ruler is to look at the men he has around him," he writes, then hammers the point: if those men are loyal, skilled, and governed by clear incentives, the state thrives even when its prince travels or falls ill. In real-estate empires, the modern equivalent of those lieutenants is the property-management corps—on-site teams, regional supervisors, third-party firms. They collect the tribute, maintain the fortresses, soothe the populace, and warn of brewing unrest. Hand this job to fools or knaves and your carefully stacked capital crumbles faster than an unwatched wall. Hand it to disciplined professionals shaped by the right incentives and your empire runs on near-autopilot, compounding wealth while you hunt fresh territories.

This chapter drills down on three pillars of Machiavellian delegation: how to choose managers, how to keep them hungry yet honest, and how to rotate and intervene before habits sour into sabotage.

I. Choosing Managers: The Filtering Crucible

1. Clarify the Mandate Before You Recruit

Machiavelli chided princes who issued vague orders, noting that hazy authority invites disobedience. Before you interview a single candidate, distill your mandate to a sentence:

"Protect net operating income, preserve building systems, and elevate tenant satisfaction—simultaneously and without excuse."

Frame every screening question against that yardstick. If a nominee's past decisions, temperament, or references clash with any clause, strike them.

2. Hunt Specialists, Not Generic Administrators

National firms boast portfolio scale, but scale alone is useless if their regional office has never managed mid-century garden multifamily in a rent-controlled borough. Demand proof they have conquered your specific asset class, demographic, and regulatory terrain. Ask for:

- A sample operating budget from a comparable building—including line-item actuals against projections.

- A copy of their internal capital-improvement playbook.

- Testimonials from two owners who still employ them after five years.

Watch for hesitation. Machiavelli's warning that "men in general judge more from appearances than from reality" applies here: shiny pitch decks can mask thin expertise.

3. Conduct a Battlefield Simulation

The résumé is rhetoric; scenarios reveal reflex. Present a live-fire drill in the interview:

> *"A water main ruptures Saturday at 3 a.m. Units on two floors flood. The fire-watch system shorts. Outline your first four phone calls, your communication to tenants, and your budget triage."*

Grade not only the steps but the tempo. Competence shows in sequencing (safety, mitigation, documentation, insurance) and in calm urgency—Machiavellian virtù under stress.

4. Leverage Network Intelligence

Just as Renaissance princes hired spies, you tap industry back-channels. Call ex-employers unlisted on the reference sheet, scan litigation dockets, scour social media. If a manager boasts of occupancy miracles yet prior owners sue for fraud, bow out politely. Reputation is predictive data.

5. Red-Flag Indicators

- **Owner-like ego.** A manager who describes *your* building as "my property" without irony may resist directives.

- **High staff turnover.** Frequent exodus signals poor leadership or under-resourced sites.

- **One-size processes.** Firms wedded to inflexible SOPs can't adapt when your asset shifts strategy.

Reject early; "injuries," Machiavelli notes, "should be inflicted all at once." Better a swift "no" than contractual entanglement.

II. Incentivizing Managers: Aligning Hunger with Honor

1. Base Pay as Table Stakes, Bonuses as Spear Points

A prince supplies his captains with rations predictable enough to prevent desperation yet lean enough that campaign booty matters. Translate that doctrine:

- **Competitive salary** ensures professionalism and reduces side-hustle distraction.

- **Performance bonuses** tied tightly to NOI growth, delinquency reduction, and tenant-satisfaction surveys convert ambition into alchemy.

Whenever possible, delay bonus payout until twelve months after the measurement period, contingent on financials maintaining target levels. This discourages short-term gloss—think deferred maintenance hidden behind cosmetic quick fixes.

2. Equity Slivers for Commanders, Not Entire Battalions

Senior regional directors who oversee clusters of stabilized assets earn phantom equity or promote-carried interests in refinances. The stake is small—2 to 5 percent—but psychologically massive. It seeds loyalty deeper than salary ever could. Frontline coordinators do not need equity; they need achievable quarterly bonuses. Lift the visionaries, feed the infantry.

3. Autonomy Corridors Bounded by Guardrails

Micromanaging every service call strangles initiative, yet unbounded discretion breeds waste. Craft a *delegated-authority matrix*:

- **Tier 1:** site manager approves repairs ≤ $500 without consultation.

- **Tier 2:** regional signs off on cap-ex between $501 and $5,000.

- **Tier 3:** ownership approval for anything above or structural.

These corridors empower swift action while flagging costly decisions for senior review. They echo Machiavelli's model city walls—pierced by gates, watched by sentries.

4. Public Recognition Programs

Praise counts as currency. Post leaderboards—time-to-complete work orders, renewal rates, utility-savings percentages—in the ops portal. Celebrate champions in quarterly town-halls. Ego is a renewable motivator; wield it.

5. The Negative Incentive: Swift, Visible Consequences

Machiavelli taught rulers to punish conspicuously to deter imitators. When a manager falsifies a ledger or ignores life-safety violations, terminate publicly within the company, document cause, and, if fraud, pursue restitution. One firm eviction fortifies the whole chain of command.

III. Policing Managers: Oversight Without Suffocation

1. Segregation of Duties—Your Dual-Key Safe

No single employee should control vendor selection, invoice approval, and payment release. Require two signatures or platform permissions in all three stages. Back-office staff rotate approvals weekly so collusion cannot root.

2. Unscheduled Audits

Quarterly audits are predictable; corruption adapts. Add randomized spot checks: reconcile petty-cash logs, pull five leases, and verify deposits hit the right escrow accounts. Machiavelli's spies appeared without warning; your auditors mirror them.

3. Digital Breadcrumbs Everywhere

Mandate cloud-based work-order systems, key-fob logins, and vendor e-payments. Manual processes invite erasure. Data trails transform suspicion into evidence—or exoneration.

4. Tenant Feedback Loops as Early-Warning Radar

Give residents a frictionless whistleblower channel: anonymous form, hotline, QR code in mailrooms. Small complaints often expose systemic rot early: unlogged service requests, cash-only late-fee transactions, harassment. Follow up within 48 hours; false alarms are cheap, missed abuse expensive.

5. Vendor Rotation and Reverse-Bid Platforms

Managers who steer work to cousins or kickback partners hollow profit. Rotate key vendors annually or run sealed e-bids that auto-rank by cost, reviews, and SLA compliance. Independence keeps the moat around owner capital.

6. Policing Sellers Under Post-Closing Occupancy

When acquisitions include seller lease-backs or repair obligations, embed inspection rights and escrow holdbacks. Property managers enforce deadlines; release draws only after photo-verified milestones. A prince never trusts a conquered lord unsupervised.

IV. Rotating Command to Prevent Complacency

1. The Entropy of Long Tenure

Managers immersed in one property for too long grow blind to incremental decay—yellowed hallway paint, half-working motion lights. They befriend tenants, relax rent-collection rigor, ignore small breaches. Machiavelli saw similar rot in provinces left to hereditary governors who "conciliate more friends than the prince."

2. Scheduled Rotation Model

- **Three-Year Tenure Ceiling.** After 36 months, move the manager to a fresh asset type: from workforce housing to mixed-use, from suburban to urban.

- **Buddy Transfer.** Promote an assistant alongside them for continuity of institutional memory; fresh eyes meet stored wisdom.

- **Cross-Training Curriculum.** Before rotation, managers attend a two-week boot camp on new building systems (steam boilers, slick roofs, POS in retail bays). Knowledge gaps shrink, confidence grows.

3. Rotation as Cultural Vaccination

Incoming managers bring best practices; outgoing managers carry lessons to their next site. The asset base evolves via horizontal pollination rather than top-down mandates. Innovation spreads like viral antibodies against complacency.

4. Handling Resident Anxiety

Tenants may panic when a beloved superintendent leaves. Announce rotations as promotions, host meet-and-greet pizza nights with incoming staff, and reassure residents that policies hold steady. People fear uncertainty more than change; fill the void with narrative.

5. Emergency Reassignment Clause

Retain contractual right to reassign managers immediately upon safety lapses, fraud suspicion, or catastrophic customer-service breaches. List specific triggers—fire-system downtime, collections below 90 percent month-to-date—to pre-empt debate. When the keep smolders, new captains sprint to the parapets.

V. Metrics That Trigger Intervention

1. The KPI Arsenal

Build a dashboard that updates daily or weekly, accessible to ownership 24/7. Core metrics include:

- **Economic Occupancy** – rent actually collected divided by gross potential. Threshold: drop below 92 percent for two consecutive months and alert fires.

- **Work-Order Closure Time** – hours from ticket open to completion. Threshold: average above 72 hours in any week.

- **Renewal Ratio** – percentage of expiring leases that renew. Threshold: dip below 45 percent in stabilized market.

- **Delinquency Rate** – dollars >30 days late as share of billed rent. Threshold: exceed 4 percent.

- **Expense-Variance** – YTD actual vs budget. Threshold: 8 percent over on controllables triggers spending freeze.

- **Mystery-Shop Score** – secret-shopper ranking on phone responsiveness, tour quality, and staff professionalism. Threshold: <80 percent leads to retraining mandate.

- **Risk Flags** – OSHA or fire-code citations. Threshold: any serious violation triggers immediate HQ site visit.

2. Dynamic Thresholds

Not all assets share standards. Student housing in May naturally posts low occupancy; luxury towers tolerate tighter variance bands. Assign property-specific control limits and review quarterly. KPIs without context mislead—like medieval scouts misreading camp-fires for army size.

3. The Intervention Ladder

1. **Yellow Flag – Remote Coaching.** Manager submits root-cause memo within 48 hours and corrective plan within five days.

2. **Orange Flag – On-Site Audit.** Regional director arrives unannounced; conducts lease audit, vendor review, tenant-focus group.

3. **Red Flag – Management Change.** Triggered by fraud, repeated KPI breaches, or safety negligence. Interim task-force parachutes in for 30 days while permanent replacement nominated.

Document each step meticulously. Process legitimacy deters allegations of unfairness—Machiavelli's prescribed shield against hatred.

4. Predictive Composite Scoring

Feed all KPIs into a weighted index—call it *Stability Score*—ranging 0–100. Machine-learn weighting based on historical pain: maybe expense variance predicts crises better than occupancy in your portfolio. When the score drops below 65, algorithm emails ownership and regional VP. Intervention starts before crisis metastasizes.

5. Tenant-Sentiment Pulse

Quarterly text surveys—*How likely are you to renew?*—provide emotional context. A falling sentiment trend often precedes delinquency spikes. Like murmurs in a medieval marketplace, early whispers guide the prince's patrols.

VI. Case Chronicles: Triumphs and Failures in Command

1. Triumph – The Manager Who Doubled NOI

A Century-old textile mill converted to loft apartments suffered 25 percent vacancy and ballooning utilities. The new manager implemented LED retrofits, re-negotiated vendor contracts, and launched a resident art-gallery program that sparked local press. Economic occupancy hit 97 percent, concessions vanished, utilities dropped 17 percent—NOI doubled in 18 months. Incentive: 10 percent of incremental NOI for two years, capped at $75 k. Ownership gladly paid it.

2. Failure – The Friend of Tenants

In a workforce-housing garden complex, a long-tenured manager forgave late fees and "worked with people" off-books. Delinquency ballooned from 3 percent to 14 percent, work-order backlogs tripled, and word spread that rules were optional. Audit uncovered cash rent payments never deposited. Replacement required eviction wave, police escorts, and $180 k bad-debt write-off. Contingency hiring saved the day—rotation would have prevented the rot.

3. Recovery – Tech Overhaul After Cyber Breach

A suburban property used outdated desktop software; manager clicked a phishing email and ransomware locked rent-payment data. Because the owner had mandated weekly cloud backups and cyber insurance, restoration finished within 36 hours, and tenant credits totaled only $6 k. Insurance covered most costs. The manager kept her job but underwent mandatory cyber-hygiene training; KPIs now include *Phishing-Simulation Pass Rate*.

VII. Synthesizing Machiavellian Delegation

A prince, Machiavelli insists, must "delegate unpopular duties" but keep "favors in his own hands." For the real-estate ruler, that means property managers chase rent and enforce rules, while ownership dispenses capital upgrades, community events, holiday bonuses. Managers absorb the friction; the owner basks in goodwill. Yet delegation is not abdication. Layered incentives, relentless surveillance, periodic rotation, and pre-agreed metrics ensure the right hand never forgets who wields the scepter.

Closing Reflection

Great kings are remembered not just for battles but for the stewards who kept cities humming between wars. Likewise, real-estate fortunes last when property managers act as disciplined stewards, their ambition fused to yours by transparent metrics and agile oversight. Choose them with care, fire them without hesitation, rotate them before they stagnate, and measure them constantly. Do this and you transform a fragile empire into a self-healing organism—one that thrives whether you are on-site or oceans away, plotting the next conquest Machiavelli would surely applaud.

Chapter 8 – Managing Reputation—Your Most Valuable Intangible

Prologue: The Echo Before the Trumpet

Machiavelli tells us that a prince "ought above all things to live with his people in such a way that no circumstance, either of prosperity or adversity, shall make him change." Reputation is that constant. Long before inspectors step through a lobby or lenders study a balance sheet, they have already decided—quietly, subconsciously—what kind of ruler you are. A Google review, a zoning-board whisper, a CRE broker's hallway aside: these form the invisible portrait against which every future request, every unexpected crisis, will be judged. Win the framing early and you borrow credibility in moments of doubt. Lose it and you fight uphill, even when facts are on your side.

This chapter teaches how to cultivate, defend, and weaponize that intangible capital across three arenas: public opinion, official favor, and financial esteem. We will then drill crisis drills—mold, crime, macro-shocks—and close with tactics for seizing narrative before rivals can tell your story for you.

Part I – Online Reviews, Local-Government Goodwill, Lender Perceptions

1. The Digital Mirror: Reviews and Ratings

"Men in general judge more by the eye than by the hand, for everyone can see and few can feel." Today the "eye" is a five-star scale shimmering on phones. One-star rants travel faster than eviction notices; glowing praise lingers like perfume. Control the mirror by designing experiences that trigger positive emotion at exactly the moments tenants reach for keyboards.

Key touchpoints

- **Move-in day.** A scented, spotless unit; a handwritten card; Wi-Fi credentials printed on stylish cardstock. Tenants snap photos, post them. Momentum gained in minute one.

- **First maintenance call.** Reply within an hour, fix within 24. Follow-up text: "Is everything perfect?" When they answer yes, send link: "Would you mind sharing that with neighbors looking for a home?"

- **Renewal anniversary.** Small rent bump delivered alongside a personal note referencing last year's improvement (new dog park, faster gate). Tenant feels progress, not extortion. Progress gets four stars; extortion gets one.

Automate review-request cadences through your property-management software, but add human follow-through. A system may send reminders; a manager's personal thank-you multiplies completion rate.

2. Government Goodwill: The Side Door to Advantage

"It is necessary for a prince, if he wants to maintain himself, to learn how not to be good, and to use this knowledge or not to use it according to necessity." "Not being good," here, can simply mean bypassing red-tape bottlenecks by having already paid political goodwill in advance. Inspectors ease up when they know your buildings exceed code by custom; planning boards smile when you fund scholarships at the community college without fanfare.

Five acts that buy grace

1. **Blight bullets.** Adopt a derelict lot near your holdings, mow it monthly, plant perennials. City officials field fewer complaint calls; they remember who solved the headache.

2. **Quarterly coffee with code enforcement.** Invite the supervisor to tour your cleanest property; ask what legislative changes loom. Knowledge exchange equals flattery; later, your permit sits atop the pile.

3. **Sponsor junior-sports gear or a neighborhood cleanup.** Modest dollars, oversized social-media resonance. Local reporters attend; you become shorthand for "engaged owner."

4. **Offer pro-bono real-estate workshops at city hall.** Show first-time buyers how to read HUD-1s. Educates voters; associates your brand with empowerment, not eviction.

5. **Lobby softly.** When text of a new housing ordinance appears, provide data, not demands. "Here is how the draft might inadvertently reduce affordable-unit supply." Officials crave numbers they can quote. Give them numbers; they give you listening-time.

3. Lender Perception: The Capital Arbiters

Banks and debt-funds replicate feudal courts: rumor can strangle a deal before underwriting begins. A single mismanaged asset can brand you "high touch" and push spread quotes wide. Build a lender dossier thicker than your loan package:

- **Quarterly portfolio memo.** One page per asset—occupancy, DSCR, renovation milestones, headwinds, next-step strategy. Email to every debt partner, even if covenants don't require it. They see transparency → lower risk premium.

- **Covenant obedience.** Treat thresholds as hard floors, not guidelines. If DSCR threatens to dip because of cap-ex push, notify in advance, present mitigation. Surprises kill trust.

- **Post-closing visits.** Invite loan officers to tour upgrades annually; show not just numbers but stainless-steel appliances, new LED corridors. Visceral proof converts spreadsheets into stories they retell in credit committee.

- **Rapid reporting.** If casualty occurs—a fire in building C—call the lender before they hear from claims adjuster. Offer your action plan, photos, reserve balances. They exhale, mark file "sponsor proactive," and move on.

Machiavelli reminds that "one's own arms" are safer than mercenaries. Yet in modern finance, senior debt is a necessary mercenary legion. Keep that legion loyal by appearing low-maintenance, high-integrity, and ever-prepared.

Part II – Crisis Communication: Mold, Crime, Market Downturns

Even the best-run principality suffers disaster. The difference between shock and downfall is how the prince communicates. Machiavelli's advice—"A prince ought to take care that he never lets anything slip from his lips that is not replete with the five qualities … gravity, courage, seriousness, strength, and energy"—translates seamlessly to press releases and tenant emails.

1. Mold: The Silent Invader

Scenario: A seasonal humidity spike reveals black spots in 12 units. Tenants tweet photos: "Toxic mold at Maple View!" The local paper retweets; calls begin.

Day-zero response—five steps

1. **Own the narrative instantly.** Public statement within three hours: "We have identified a moisture issue in a portion of Maple View. Certified remediation teams are on-site. Health and safety are our top priority."

2. **Show action visually.** Post images of technicians in Tyvek suits sealing vents. Optics quell panic.

3. **Offer relocation and vouchers.** Affected tenants receive hotel plus per diem day one. Pre-negotiated rates with nearby chain reduce cost; speed buys goodwill.

4. **Deploy independent testing.** Hire third-party lab; announce results timeline publicly. Objectivity shields against "cover-up" accusations.

5. **Report progress daily.** Even "No new updates, work continues" beats silence. Absence breeds rumors; presence projects control.

Post-mortem: Publish a white paper on building-envelope lessons learned. Share with city council and green-building groups. Mistake becomes thought-leadership pivot; reputation not just recovered but expanded.

2. Crime: The Optics of Fear

Scenario: A shooting in your parking lot. Cameras catch two non-resident gangs. Media labels property "danger zone." Occupancy drops five points in a month.

Immediate protocol

- **Joint statement with police within 24 hours.** Reassure that suspects were unaffiliated, arrests imminent. Appear as partner to law enforcement, not passive landlord.

- **Set tactical timeline**:

    - **48 hours**—increase lighting lumens, add roving patrols, hold resident town-hall with precinct captain.

    - **72 hours**—install license-plate cameras; send footage of past trespassers to detectives.

    - **One week**—announce courtyard redesign eliminating blind corners; break ground within 30 days.

Narrative pivot: Launch "Safe Spaces Initiative," monthly self-defense classes, free to public. Media returns for follow-up, prints redemption arc. Machiavelli preached transformation: "A prince is also esteemed when he is a true friend and a true enemy." Take clear side with residents; be enemy to crime.

3. Market Downturn: Recession-Grade Messaging

When rents plateau and layoffs loom, the rumor mill whispers "huge rent hikes coming" or "owner will sell to slumlords." Preempt:

- **Transparency letter** to residents: "Economic conditions challenge everyone. We remain committed to moderate, predictable increases aligned with CPI. We are also enhancing referral credits to keep our community stable."

- **City-hall briefing**: Provide data on local-employment losses; propose partnership for rent-support grants. Officials who see you as proactive ally will defend you if activists call you predator.

- **Lender calls**: Present recession contingency—expense trimming, interest-rate caps already in place, occupancy cushion. Ask lenders about their stress metrics; align your reporting to calm them.

Machiavelli's counsel—"Fortune is a woman… it is necessary to hold her down"—means you grip uncertainty with confident policy, not hope.

Part III – Controlling the Narrative Before Competitors Do

1. First-Mover Advantage in Storytelling

If you don't tell your tale, rivals will write it. Competitors love to sow fear: "Their rents spike every renewal," "Maintenance never shows." Counteract with constant drip-feed of positive fact. Monthly newsletters, community-impact infographics, open-house tours for brokers—these shape perception before gossip lands.

2. Building Brand Archetype

Choose one identity and repeat relentlessly:

- **The Green Guardian**—solar arrays, compost stations, electric-vehicle chargers.

- **The Heritage Restorer**—historic façades, art walks, local artisans.

- **The Tech Haven**—gig-fiber, smart locks, coworking hubs.

Archetype guides every social-post, press interview, sponsorship. Competitors trying to smear you must fight a clear, deeply planted image.

3. Programming Reputation Pipelines

- **Media Calendar**: Pre-draft twelve press releases annually—quarterly financial milestones, new amenities, philanthropy. Even if no paper prints, posts live on your site, feeding search engines.

- **Broker Webinars**: Quarterly Zoom on submarket trends. Position yourself as data source; brokers repeat your statistics at cocktail events.

- **Resident Ambassador Program**: Identify five enthusiastic tenants per asset; comp them $25 rent credit for quarterly blog post or Instagram reel about living there. Authentic voices drown out malcontents.

4. Social Listening Command Center

Monitor brand mentions via Google Alerts, Reddit, Nextdoor. Set threshold: negative sentiment spike of 30 percent triggers response team within two hours. Use templated triage questions—What claim? Photo evidence? Which address?—to move conversation from public feed to private resolution quickly.

5. Preemptive Myth Busting

Publish FAQ micro-videos:

- "Why your rent increases 3%—breakdown of property-tax hikes and insurance costs."

- "Where your amenity fee goes—pools tested twice daily, gym equipment serviced monthly."

Transparency thwarts rumor before it blooms.

6. Partnership Shields

Join industry and civic associations: apartment associations, chambers of commerce, neighborhood alliances. When critics accuse you of profiteering, third-party leaders can vouch for your collaboration track record. As Machiavelli notes, "A prince best secures himself when he is supported by the great." In modern times, "the great" may be a respected nonprofit director.

Part IV – Reputation Flywheel Case Studies

Case: Turning a 2.6 Google Rating into 4.4 in Nine Months

Problem: Decade-old student housing plagued by maintenance delays, noisy parties, low stars. Competitor across campus touted modern tower, threatened mass exodus.

Plan:

1. **Rapid-response task-force** closed 400 work orders in 30 days.

2. **Noise amnesty event**: Resident assistants collected anonymous party-house addresses; management installed soundproof door sweeps.

3. **Gamified review drive**: Each five-star review earned building-wide pizza slice tally; 100 slices = free courtyard concert.

Outcome: Stars rose quarterly: 2.6 → 3.1 → 3.8 → 4.4. Occupancy regained 96%. Competitor's smear flyers backfired; students posted rebuttals citing visible upgrades. Lesson: fix root causes first, then mobilize satisfied voices.

Case: Leveraging Local Government Favor to Win Expansion Approval

Problem: Needed rezoning from light-industrial to mixed-use, facing neighborhood opposition claiming "traffic nightmare."

Strategy:

- Conducted **volunteer traffic counts** at peak times, discovered city signal timings outdated.

- Offered to **fund smart-signal upgrade** if project approved.

- Hosted **public design charrette**; added bike lanes, public plaza.

Result: Planning commission voted 7-0 for rezoning. Councilmember quoted developer's willingness to "invest in solving legacy congestion." Competitors who hoped denial would guard their rents lost field.

When lockdown slashed small-retail tenants, owner's NOI plunged 22%. Rather than wait for covenant breach letter, CEO held **weekly Zoom** with bank team, sharing lease-by-lease rent-relief status and reopening forecasts. Provided **tenant-credit dashboards**; invited lender's analyst to site walkthrough via live video. Bank waived DSCR for four quarters, praised owner's transparency in earnings call. Competitors defaulted; their assets sold at discount. Reputation literally bought time.

Part V – Practical Toolkit for Sustained Esteem

1. **Reputation Runway Spreadsheet**—log all goodwill initiatives, assign ROI estimate, renewal-rate impact, and media reach. Reviews intangible become trackable.

2. **Crisis-copy vault**—pre-approved templates for mold, violence, eviction moratoriums, construction accidents. Speed trumps wordsmithing during chaos.

3. **Stakeholder Map**—color-code influence: tenants (green), officials (blue), lenders (gray), media (purple). Update quarterly with sentiment scores, last-contact date, next-action note.

4. **Shadow Search Audit**—incognito Google search on company and property names monthly; screenshot page one. Watch progress from neutral results to curated positives.

5. **Reputation Insurance**—yes, it exists. Policies cover crisis-PR firm fees. Premiums drop if you show active risk-mitigation protocols; your programs pay for themselves.

Epilogue: The Covenant of Perception

Machiavelli's Italy teemed with plotting nobles spinning tales to legitimize coups. Our digital century is no gentler: a disgruntled tenant's TikTok can reach a million in hours. But the Florentine's core is still true: "Good counsel, whencesoever it comes, ought to be accepted." Good counsel here means constant self-audit of the stories whispering about you. Accept the feedback, adjust the reality, then edit the rumor mill before it prints.

Cultivated reputation becomes a defensive moat, a competitive sword, and, during crises, a reserve currency. Treat it like any other asset—budget for it, insure it, monitor it—and one day you will find bankers quoting your newsletters, councilmembers praising your lighting upgrades, and prospective tenants arriving already convinced that no safer, fairer kingdom exists. That is the measure of an invisible capital turned tangible: prosperity that precedes your arrival and lingers long after the meeting ends, securing the principality of your portfolio for cycles to come.

Chapter 9 – Strategic Alliances with Brokers, Lenders, and Officials

Prelude: A League of Interests

Machiavelli's pages thrum with alliances—Florentine merchants who grease a duke's campaigns, papal bankers who bankroll near-impossible sieges, city-state envoys trading favors that echo for decades. He cautions that "the friendship which is bought with money, and not by greatness and nobility of character, is not bought, but may be sold." Translation for the modern investor: partnerships must grow from shared incentives, not from desperation cheques or hollow titles. When the bond is rooted in genuinely aligned gain, it outlives cycles and crises; when it rests on a one-off transaction, it snaps at the first shake of fortune's wheel.

This chapter shows how to forge and steward three categories of strategic ally—brokers, lenders, and government actors—so that each sees your success as their own. We then dig into the subtle art of offering tiny—but perfectly timed—favors that accumulate into heavy influence. Finally, we draw the line between handshake coalitions and formal, paper-sealed partnerships, because power can calcify as easily as it expands.

I. Crafting Mutually Beneficial Pacts

1. Brokers: The Scouts and Heralds of the Realm

Brokers speak to everyone—competitors, buyers, sellers, bureaucrats—and so function as the principality's external sensory system. The prince who fields trusted scouts hears rumors while they are still whispers.

Designing the pact

1. **Speed-of-response covenant** – Promise a decision on every opportunity they send within forty-eight hours. Your quick thumbs-up or pass keeps their pipeline moving; they reward you with first look at the choicest deals.

2. **Certainty-of-close pledge** – Back letters of intent with hard deposits and pre-vetted financing. Nothing converts a broker's loyalty like seeing their commission wired exactly on schedule.

3. **Data feedback loop** – After closing, share leasing velocity, rent deltas, and exit cap targets (scrubbed of sensitive numbers). Brokers feed on data; by enriching them you enhance their credibility in other rooms—all roads leading back to you.

4. **Joint-narrative marketing** – Invite the broker to co-author a local-media op-ed or webinar on submarket trends. Their brand rises, your thought-leadership halo expands, and the next wave of sellers tags both of you as the dream team.

Machiavelli notes, "The wise man does at once what the fool does finally." Render broker-friendly terms before they ask; they will knight you as preferred client long before rival suitors finish diligence.

2. Lenders: The Lords of Liquidity

To Machiavelli, foreign mercenaries were dangerous but often necessary. Senior debt is your mercenary legion—highly potent, sometimes fickle, always pivotal.

Designing the pact

1. **Transparency covenant** – Quarterly KPI dashboards delivered without being chased. The lender's biggest pain is chasing documents; remove that friction and you graduate from commodity borrower to golden goose.

2. **Pre-emptive risk sharing** – If coverage ratios tighten, alert them first. Propose injecting fresh equity or escrowing six months' interest up front. You transform from monitored counterparty to proactive co-strategist.

3. **Portfolio-wide mandate** – Offer them the inside track on your entire pipeline for the next twelve months, but with no exclusivity. They glimpse volume upside; you retain freedom. This "first call but not last word" format flatters without handcuffs.

4. **Event hospitality** – Host lender-only tours of award-winning rehabs, followed by moderated panels on property technology. Their analysts gain case-study ammo

for credit committee. You're now not a supplicant, but an educator of capital.

3. Officials: The Gatekeepers of Entitlements

Permits, zoning variances, and public sentiment all route through humans in office. Court them the Machiavellian way—never bribery, always enlightened self-interest visible to the electorate they serve.

Designing the pact

1. **Problem-solver brand** – Quarterly, email a one-page policy memo about improving housing code efficiency: fewer inspection delays, digital permit uploads. Offer pilots in your buildings. Officials leverage your pilot to tout modernization.

2. **Community capital fund** – Create a micro-grant pool (say, $25 000 a year) for neighborhood beautification. Let city council allocate recipients; you merely cut the cheque and spotlight their choice. They receive public praise, you receive their introductions when new land assemblages surface.

3. **Crisis resource alignment** – Offer your vacant units as temporary shelter during natural disasters or domestic-violence relocations. You set strict time limits and liability coverage, but the gesture lodges your name in every emergency-management meeting.

4. **Neutral data clearinghouse** – Provide anonymized tenant turnover data to planning departments exploring demographic trends. They cite your report in hearings—each citation enhancing your stance as civic partner.

"Men sooner forget the death of their father than the loss of their patrimony," Machiavelli quips. Help officials guard *their* patrimony—votes and public acclaim—and they will guard your projects in return.

II. Using Small Favors to Gain Leverage

1. The Psychology of Micro-Obligation

Humans tally debts of gratitude with extraordinary precision. An expedited notary stamp, a last-minute conference-room loan, a congratulatory tweet amplified at midnight—such gestures stick inside memory like barbs. The recipient may never repay overtly, but the tilt remains, inclining later decisions subconsciously in your favor. Machiavelli advises that a prince should distribute "little benefits" continuously, saving grand gifts for crises.

2. Tactical Favor Playbook

- **Broker resumé booster** – After a deal closes, write a two-paragraph testimonial and post on LinkedIn tagging the broker's principal. Ten minutes of your time; months of inbound leads for them. Later, when a pocket listing surfaces, guess who phones you first?

- **Lender reputational shield** – Provide an on-the-record quote praising their reliability to an industry journalist. Lending officers crave positive press seldom offered by borrowers. When spreads tick up next quarter, they slip you a waiver or lower-fee term for the mission-critical refinance.

- **Official's pet project** – An alderwoman wants bike racks near your retail strip. Approve overnight at your expense; cost is negligible versus months shaved off your signage permit.

- **Holiday micro-gifts** – Instead of generic baskets, send a custom metric: "Your closed-deal throughput with us in 2025 saved 14 days underwriting on average—here's a framed infographic." People display data trophies on desks; each glance re-seals allegiance.

3. Timing and Authenticity

The favor loses magic if transactional haze is visible. Offer spontaneously, ideally minutes after discovering the need, with no request attached. Machiavelli: "A benefit should be conferred gradually; and thus it will taste better." Spread micro-benefits like breadcrumbs; the path leads back to your conference table when big decisions ripen.

4. Reciprocity Ratchet

Track favors in a private ledger, not to demand payback but to pace them. Too many gifts too fast look like bribery; too sparse and the chain of goodwill rusts. Aim for one unobtrusive assist per quarter per core ally, more only in active project crunches.

III. When to Formalize Partnerships vs. Stay Independent

1. Partnership Spectrum

- **Loose handshake** – No contract, shared intent only (e.g., "You get first look at our dispositions").

- **Memorandum of Understanding** – Non-binding bullet-points of each side's roles, signed but not litigable.

- **Joint Venture Agreement** – Equity sharing, waterfall, control clauses, exit triggers.

- **Framework Agreement** – Master funding facility or broker-of-record pact covering multiple assets with renewals.

2. Decision Drivers

1. **Capital intensity and uniqueness** – Massive adaptive-reuse needing $100 M senior + mezz? Formalize. Simple value-add in plentiful submarket? Stay flexible.

2. **Regulatory risk** – Projects hinging on city-council votes favor written coalition with local civic trust, locking them as co-GP to prove community stakes.

3. **Repetition horizon** – If you foresee ten deals over five years with the same broker, a framework agreement codifies commission scales and exclusivity radius, reducing friction.

4. **Exit optionality** – Partnerships limit unilateral sale. If market signals fast flip, independent stance lets you pivot. Assess your likely liquidity window before signing away control.

3. Machiavellian Caution

"Alliances made by desertion are never reliable," the Florentine warns. Translate: if a prospective partner is ditching a current ally to join you, watch their loyalty. Past behavior indicates future exit velocity.

4. Drafting the Un-Romantic Clauses

- **Deadlock breakers** – Mediation → buy-sell shotgun → forced liquidation.

- **Key-man triggers** – If specific broker leaves firm, exclusivity dissolves.

- **Performance hurdles** – Lender may demand DSCR or pace-of-draw milestones; codify remedies early.

- **Sunset dates** – Alliances, like crops, require harvest cycles. A three-year automatic expiration with mutual-renewal clause prevents lingering commitments mismatched to new market realities.

5. Independence Insurance

When you *do* formalize, keep at least one alternate channel open—another brokerage relationship, a standby credit facility, a zoning attorney outside the primary circle. Machiavelli's prince cultivated auxiliary troops; if primary legions falter, reinforcements deter blackmail.

IV. Field Tactics: Three Real-World Coalition Stories

1. Off-Market Trophy via Broker Blood-Oath

A midwestern multifamily operator answered every one of a particular broker's emails inside 30 minutes for two years, even on dead leads. The loyalty impression ran so deep that when a 300-unit Class A owner whispered interest before listing, the broker walked straight past bigger-fee national investors and gave the lead to the operator *exclusively*. They offered full ask, signed PSA in five days, retraded zero dollars. Broker earned full commission and immortal gratitude; operator gained flagship asset. No contract bound them—only habitual responsiveness.

2. Lender Flex Clause Saves Conversion

During pandemic, construction lender balked at condo sales velocity. Borrower had fed weekly drone-footage updates and transparent budget overruns for months, building trust. Bank agreed to convert unsold units into rental hold, modifying loan to five-year mini-perm at minimal fee. Comparable developers without disclosure discipline hit maturity default. Pact paid off in breathing room, all because credibility reserves were full.

3. City-Hall Alliance Wins Height Variance

A developer funded $50 000 STEM scholarships administered by city foundation. A year later they sought a two-story height variance for downtown infill. Public-meeting opponents cried shadow and traffic. City education board testified in favor, praising scholarship pipeline. Council passed variance 6-1. Scholarships cost 0.2% of project budget, returned millions in extra sellable square footage. The favor planted early sprouted precisely on zoning-vote day.

V. Implementation Blueprint

1. **Stakeholder grid** – List each key broker, lender officer, councilmember. Add columns: personal motivators, last favor given, next value opportunity, formalization status.

2. **Quarterly alliance review** – Ask: Have mutual gains grown? Are we too dependent? Should we document roles?

3. **Favor calendar** – Schedule micro-gifts against birthdays, fiscal year-ends, or council election cycles for maximum resonance.

4. **Risk scan** – At each review, brainstorm "If ally exits/turns, what's Plan B?" Maintain secondary contacts before Plan B is needed.

Epilogue: The Compass of Shared Incentive

In one of his starkest lines, Machiavelli reminds us that "goodwill is gained by other things than killing and plundering." The real-estate prince prospers through coalitions that feel so equitable, so repeatable, that participants defend the alliance out of enlightened self-interest. Brokers guard your reputation because it feeds theirs. Lenders champion your underwriting because it proves their risk models. Officials expedite your permits because your projects buttress their voter narrative.

Cultivate that intersection of motives, reinforce it with small but unforgettable favors, and formalize only when the ledger of pros and cons says permanence beats agility. Do this, and every expansion you attempt will ride into the arena flanked by scouts, bankers, and civic banner-bearers already singing your virtues—while rivals, isolated and under-networked, scramble to book the opening act.ज्ज

Chapter 10 – Neutralizing Competitors and Naysayers

Prelude: The Field of Invisible Daggers

Machiavelli warned that a prince who conquers new territory "must live there" or risk losing it to lurking enemies. In property markets, you rarely "live" inside every parcel—you rely on contracts and managers—so flanking forces multiply. Rival investors watch the same MLS alerts, offer on the same distressed notes, court the same aldermen. Activists shout "gentrifier," union leaders protest conversions, jealous brokers leak half-truths.

Neutralizing these threats does **not** mean scorched-earth aggression. "The injuries," Machiavelli counsels, "must be inflicted once for all," while benefits "must be conferred little by little." Your task: strike quickly, legally, and decisively when rivals threaten your flank—then lay steady groundwork that turns yesterday's foe into tomorrow's auxiliary. This chapter weaves three battlefronts:

1. **Competitive intelligence**—mapping every acquisition, capital raise, and municipal hearing your rivals touch.

2. **Legal hardball**—assertive yet defensible tactics that sap a competitor's momentum without flirting with antitrust or tort traps.

3. **Co-option**—alchemy that rebadges a competitor's talents as your joint-venture horsepower.

Part I – Competitive Intelligence: Tracking Rival Acquisitions

1. Why Watch the Board?

Machiavelli accuses unprepared rulers of "fortune's blind victims," reacting only after schemes mature. The modern blind ruler says, *"Wow, when did they buy six lots on the Green Line?"* A live intel feed flips reactivity to pre-emption; you swing bids a week earlier, file liens before rezoning, or pivot asset classes before cap-rate spreads compress.

2. Building the Radar Grid

Clerk-file sweeps – Script weekly scrapes of county recorder databases for deed transfers above predetermined price-per-square-foot. Tag entities; cross-reference with LLC parent registries to unmask shell buyers.

Permit cloud – Suburban competitors quietly stockpile duplex lots? Pull building-permit apps daily; filter for addresses inside their known ZIPs. A spike flags a secret rollout before press releases trumpet groundbreakings.

Debt-market sniffers – Track UCC filings and securitized-loan dashboards. When a rival collateralizes a portfolio, you know their leverage ratio, term sheet, and maturity cliff—perfect timing for a predatory offer when they breach covenants later.

Broker couriers – Cultivate junior brokers, title closers, even signage installers. Each sees deals weeks before market. A $500 gift card following every confirmed whisper keeps their phones buzzing your number first.

Public-opinion sonar – Twitter keyword strings, neighborhood Facebook groups, Nextdoor hints. Sellers brag "a big developer is sniffing around." Pin maps around chatter clusters; your acquisitions team canvasses those blocks before letters of intent fly.

3. Pattern-Recognition Playbooks

Create dossiers per rival:

- **Capital stack profile** – PE joint venture? Crowdfund? 1031 rollovers? Their cheapest capital defines the ceiling you can push them toward.

- **Signature renovation thumbprint** – Do they always add dog parks? Convert laundry rooms to Amazon lockers? Spotting patterns lets you pre-empt with your own upgrade campaign, stealing tenant hearts before they fetch rent premiums.

- **Political alliances** – Campaign-finance reports reveal which councilmember they fund. Counter by sponsoring alternative committees or, smarter, by funding the same ally to dilute exclusivity.

4. Aggressive but Ethical Ops

Busybody reconnaissance can drift unethical. Never hack emails, impersonate inspectors, or bribe officials—felonies dismantle empires. Stick to public filings, voluntary disclosures, consensual interviews, and commercially available data sets. Machiavelli reminds, "The ends justify the means" only if the means don't hand enemies a dagger called "litigation."

5. Action Triggers

- **20 percent land-bank threshold** – If a rival controls one-fifth of lots in a corridor, file early stage talks with adjacent owners so they can't encircle you.

- **Three consecutive permit spikes** – Suspect stealth pivot—commission feasibility in the same use to crowd their pipeline.

- **Senior-loan maturing within 12 months and DSCR <1.15** – Approach lender with backup offer to purchase note at discount. You neutralize competitor by owning the leverage.

Part II – Legal Boundaries of Hardball Tactics

1. Strike Zones vs. Foul Balls

Hardball wins territory, but foul balls bleed cash in court. Distinguish:

- **Lawful pressure** – filing protest letters during rezoning hearings, buying option contracts that lock critical ingress easements, or legal rental-rate competition.

- **Prohibited conduct** – price-fixing, malicious defamation, tortious interference (encouraging tenants to break valid leases), or sham litigation aimed purely to delay.

Burn this line into every lieutenant's brain.

2. Weaponizing Due Process

Comment-letter sieges – During public-notice windows for a competitor's variance, submit expert reports on traffic, shadow impact, water runoff. Cite code, not emotion. The process is public; you are a stakeholder. Delay costs them interest carry; maybe they cut you into the deal.

FOIA scalpel – Freedom-of-Information requests for competitor's correspondence with planning staff expose inconsistencies. Use them in hearings to erode credibility—always deliver in calm, factual tone to avoid slander.

Right-of-first-refusal sniping – When an inclusionary-housing covenant grants tenants ROFR on condo conversions, fund tenants' legal fees to exercise. Either you step in as back-up buyer or the competitor's ROI profile implodes, forcing renegotiation.

3. Contractual Minefields

Insert **anti-assignment clauses** when you buy loan notes, preventing borrowers (i.e., competitors) from transferring interests without your consent. Insert **call options** in JV charters—if partner sells stake you dislike, you can seize at preset valuation.

Machiavelli said, "Fortresses may be useful or not, according to circumstances." Contractual fortresses cost little to build and may save you when the siege engines roll.

4. Defensive Litigation Shields

Carry **litigation-expense insurance**; aggressive posture invites counter-suits. Keep a **crisis-response file**: press template, counsel contacts, chronology log. When you serve a cease-and-desist for brand infringement, competitor's PR team receives your statement simultaneously—preventing them painting you villain first.

5. Ethical Signposts

Before green-lighting any hardball manoeuvre, run three tests:

1. **Legality** – on the books.

2. **Optics** – on the evening news.

3. **Reciprocity** – if mirrored back, can you sustain?

Machiavelli: "Men avenge slight offenses, graver ones they cannot." Strike so well within law that retaliation would appear petty or self-harmful.

Part III – Turning Competitors into Joint-Venture Partners

1. The Persuasion Pivot

Sometimes the enemy holds keys you need—local boots, entitlements, cap-ex runway. Machiavelli extols co-opting former foes: "The best fortress which a prince can possess is the affection of his people." For you, affection equals aligned returns.

Identify synergies:

- Your cheap capital + their land bank.

- Your construction team + their political inroads.

- Your asset-management tech + their leasing machine.

2. Courtship Protocol

1. **Quiet coffee** – Raise compliments: "Your lease-up pace on the South Loop deal impressed us." Ego balm resets posture.

2. **Data-sharing teaser** – Offer anonymized occupancy trend from your nearby assets. Signals abundance, not need.

3. **Pilot micro-venture** – Propose a single parcel or note purchase. Cap tables 50/50, low risk. Both sides test chemistry.

Once trust forms, escalate to multi-asset programmatic JV with waterfall aligning promote after hitting return hurdles. Legal counsel drafts exit option for either side at fair-value appraisal after five years—commitment but not prison.

3. Converting Naysayers and Activists

Opponents of densification, short-term rentals, or rent bumps thrive on exclusion narratives. Flip them:

- **Community equity slice** – Offer neighborhood association 3 percent of GP carry. Suddenly they tout "our project."

- **Workforce upskilling** – Fund local trade apprenticeships tied to your builds; union reps shift from protest to collaboration.

- **Revenue-sharing amenities** – A rooftop bar leases to local restaurateur; activists see supporting small business, not corporate greed.

Machiavelli's insight: "The people are more honest in their intentions than the nobles." Provide tangible gain; sincerity emerges.

4. JV Failure Modes and Antidotes

- **Culture clash** – One side penny-pinches, other splurges on finishes. Solution: governance board with cap-ex approval thresholds; deadlock shotgun clause.

- **Unequal bandwidth** – Smaller partner can't staff weekly site meetings. Build reimbursable management fee tiered to task load.

- **Exit paranoia** – Each fears other will dump stake at market peak. Install right of first offer plus step-down prepayment penalties on financing to deter opportunistic exits.

5. Case Snapshots

- **From bidding war to consortium** – Three groups chased a courthouse REO. Instead, they pooled: one raised debt, second handled value-add, third mastered lease-up. Shared risk, doubled speed, outperformed original pro formas.

- **Environmental liability détente** – A competitor's brownfield scare tanked their capital. You entered as 60 percent partner, brought environmental PI insurance, shared upside for cheap. They salvaged project; you gained barrier to entry.

Part IV – Toolkit for Continuous Dominance

1. **Rival dossier template** – entity chart, capital sources, political donations, public quotes.

2. **Legal-tactics decision tree** – protest, FOIA, ROFR funding, note purchase.

3. **Favor ledger** – track micro gestures to potential JV converts; note next soft touch.

4. **JV scorecard** – evaluate proposals on synergy %, control rights, IRR delta over solo path.

Epilogue: The Unseen Edges

From the Florentine's vantage, a prince who sees farther than neighbors and captures minds before blades rarely needs war.

Your kingdom of deeds and cap rates likewise prospers when rivals exhaust themselves reacting to puzzles you solved yesterday. Track them quietly, fence them lawfully, invite them profitably, and you become what Machiavelli called **"the lion and the fox"—strength married to cunning**. The market's whispers shift: first grudging respect, then wary cooperation, finally reluctant dependence. By then the battlefield of competitors and naysayers has become your supply chain.

Chapter 11 – Scaling the Empire Without Overstretch

Opening Frame: Growth as Double-Edged Sword

Machiavelli lectured that a prince who expands too rapidly "will incur the hatred of many and the friendship of few, and he will not stand long." His Renaissance warning translates cleanly to property empires: grow without discipline and leverage mutates from fuel to fuse, geographical sprawl dilutes oversight, and the very acclaim that once opened city-hall doors morphs into populist scrutiny. This chapter sets the governor on the engine—three throttles that prevent flash-burn: precision debt sizing, brutal stress-testing, and calculated geographic diversification; a delegation lattice of regional viceroys that retains Machiavellian unity of command; and, finally, the humility to call time-out when variables tilt beyond the portfolio's design envelope.

I. Debt Sizing, Risk Stress-Tests, Geographic Diversification

1. Debt Sizing—The Golden Ratio of Power and Peril

"He who depends wholly on fortune will ruin himself when she changes." Since leverage amplifies fortune, you must engineer the margin that survives her mood swings. Start by rejecting percentage formulas scraped from blogs. One asset's safe 70 percent loan-to-value may be lethal for another if exposure layers—construction risk atop reposition risk atop refinance risk. Instead, debt capacity emerges from three lenses: volatility of income, liquidity of collateral, and refinancing outlook.

Volatility lens

 • Class A downtown office rents float on economic tides; require fixed-rate amortizing debt and fifteen-year term.
 • Section 8 multifamily funded by government vouchers? Revenue volatility is low; interest-only agency debt at higher leverage can still clear stress DSCR thresholds.

Liquidity lens

 • Self-storage trades every week on a national exchange of 1031 hunters; high liquidity lowers forced-sale haircut, justifying leverage uptick.
 • Rural senior housing at two-star licensing? Liquidity razor-thin—debt should glide no higher than 55 percent.

Refinance lens

 • If exit refinance date lands in the same fiscal year when $300 billion of CMBS maturities swell supply, assume spreads 50 basis points wider and proceed only if DSCR still >1.20.
 • Alternatively, structure a forward-rate lock or fixed-stepdown built into loan docs—pay a slight premium now for a floor under tomorrow's cost of capital.

Calculate global leverage not as simple average but as portfolio-weighted Value at Risk (VaR). If a single construction loan sits at 80 percent LTC, counterbalance with cash-flowing assets at 50 percent LTV until aggregate VaR per scenario curve meets target (<10 percent equity erosion at 99th percentile shock). Excel can crunch, but discipline decides.

2. Risk Stress-Tests—The Wargames Table

Machiavelli studied Roman legions because "in peaceful times they exercised their soldiers not less than in the time of war." Your digital troops are spreadsheets and Monte Carlo engines. Stress-test across four fronts:

Macroeconomic shock
 • Stagflation: cap rates decompress 100 bps, CPI +4 percent, job growth –2 percent.
 • Deflationary spiral: interest rates plummet but rents drop 10 percent.

Operational breakage
 • Cyber-attack locks smart-home systems; occupancy falls 5 percent while remediation costs $600 per unit.
 • Strikes at largest tenant's headquarters slash their payroll, triggering co-tenancy clauses across shopping center.

Climate and casualty events
 • Hurricane flood maps revised; insurance deductible jumps from 1 to 5 percent of value.
 • Wildfire smoke drives air-filtration retrofit at every West-coast asset, $0.40 per square foot capex.

Regulatory upheaval
 • New rent-control cap of CPI plus 1 percent; asset t-12 rent growth resets.

• City imposes vacancy tax for units empty >90 days; flips long-term vacancy loss into explicit levy.

Run each scenario at portfolio level, property level, and debt-covenant tier. Report time-to-breach: how many months before DSCR <1.10 or cash reserves <6 months OPEX? Where numbers shrink to single digits, restructure. Maybe sell a tail asset, maybe swap floating for fixed, maybe raise mezzanine to build liquidity. Wargames reveal which bastions crumble first; reinforcement happens before clouds gather.

3. Geographic Diversification—Territorial Counterweights

"Princes, in guarding their states, ought very rarely go in person to them, but they should do so on some pressing occasions." If you cannot be omnipresent, spread risk so one city's earthquake, tax revolt, or employer exodus never topples the throne.

Diversify economic drivers
 Pair tech-heavy Austin office with Kansas City logistics where e-commerce warehousing, not venture capital, rules hiring.

Diversify policy climates
 Push affordable-housing product in landlord-friendly Texas when expanding market-rate through progressive Denver. When one side clamps, the other loosens.

Diversify disaster profiles
 Allocate coastal hurricane play (insurance baked) plus inland tornado belt plus seismic West. Model aggregated natural-cat

output so annual probable-maximum-loss remains <15 percent equity.

While diversifying, maintain strategic contiguity: pick three to five "operating theaters" no further than two-hour flight where you can install regional viceroys. Forty units in Montana do nothing but pull oversight bandwidth. Either scale to economic density or exit.

II. Delegation Structures: Regional "Viceroys"

1. The Anatomy of a Viceroy

Machiavelli admired the Ottomans' provincial system: pashas governed provinces yet answered absolutely to the sultan. You replicate via regional directors who command local property managers, broker pipelines, political liaisons, but feed weekly intel to headquarters.

Powers
• Approve capex < $250 k, sign service contracts < one year, authorize market-rate rent increases within CPI+2 range.
• Represent ownership at city-council hearings, chamber-of-commerce boards, and broker walk-throughs.

Constraints
• Must hit portfolio cash yield targets and DSCR floors.
• Cannot sign debt instruments, nor file plats, without HQ legal vetting.

Accountability
 • Quarterly scorecard—economic occupancy, expense variance,
compliance audits, goodwill initiatives.
 • 360-degree reviews—on-site team, tenants, HQ. Poor culture
marks lose bonus cash.

2. Selection and Grooming

Choose local polyglots: they speak permit official dialect, lender
dialect, subcontractor dialect. Hire for five-tool skill—finance
literacy, construction sense, political charm, tech aptitude, grit.
Rotate them through different asset classes during training year:
three months shadow on infill retail, three on workforce-housing
lease-ups, three on capital markets. They graduate with macro
lens.

3. Communication Cadence and the "Central Ear"

Deploy synchronous stand-ups Monday morning; each viceroy
fields KPI anomalies. HQ analysts drill into variance and escalate
for board attention. Thursday think-tank call—viceroys share wins
so cross-pollination flows. Annual summit rotates cities; HQ
demonstrates respect by showing up on viceroy turf.

4. Succession Pipeline and Mutiny Safeguards

Clone bench: each viceroy backs up by senior ops manager. No
realm depends on one personality. If KPI index slides two
quarters, HQ triggers "governor swap." Machiavelli warned: "He
who is the cause of another becoming powerful ruins himself." A
viceroy may gather loyalties that rival HQ influence; curb that by

rotating subordinate managers across regions semi-annually and by HQ approving all promotions.

5. Tech Spine

Provide viceroys real-time dashboards: rent roll deltas, heat-map of maintenance tickets, political-risk scorecards. They need field clarity; you need transparency into their vantage. Data is leash and gift.

III. Knowing When to Slow Growth

1. The Vanity Metric Trap

Pipeline volume—letters of intent issued, press-release square footage—feels like progress. *"Men are quicker to forget the death of their father than the loss of their patrimony."* Capital markets forget your last ribbon-cutting the minute DSCR falters. Replace vanity metrics with survival indicators: unlevered yield on cost, reserve months, VaR.

2. Leading-Edge Signals to Tap the Brakes

Deal friction – Adds five days each legal review because compliance backlogs. Bottleneck signals people overstretch.
Quality drift – Work order close-out times inch above 72 hours.
Debt spreads – Your latest term-sheet premium jumps 40 bps over previous closes, a market verdict on risk.
Political backlash – Council meeting agendas fill with "moratorium," "anti-displacement," "luxury tax" referencing your

name.

Bench depletion – High performers decline promotion; HR time-to-fill expands.

Chart these metrics monthly. Define "yellow zone" thresholds; if three bells ring simultaneously, call strategic pause: freeze new LOIs, hold weekly cash-scenario model, direct viceroys to remediate operations.

3. Pause Does Not Equal Paralysis

In slowdown season:

• Complete audits and energy retrofits; push NOI through efficiency.
 • Refinance fixed at opportunistic dips; hoard liquidity.
 • Strengthen community programs; pivot PR from conquest to stewardship.
 • Plan next-cycle land-bank acquisitions via options, not closings (option fees minimal).

Like a phalanx drawing shields, you regroup, let froth bleed out of markets, and preserve agility.

4. Board Narrative

Investors fear stalls; frame pause as "Fortress Initiative Phase." Present stress-test data and credit-spread charts as reasons. Cite Machiavelli: "It is better to be cautious than impetuous, for fortune changes." Stakeholders appreciate survival mode if numbers tell the tale.

5. Restart Criteria

Set tripwire indicators:

• Loan-to-treasury spreads contract 30 bps.
 • Construction cost index plateaus two quarters.
 • Vacancy in target submarkets tightens under 6 percent.
 • Internal capacity ratio (open positions / total FTE) below 8 percent.

When three of four fire green, lift freeze gradually: first resume option exercises, then small-cap acquisitions, finally major ground-up.

Closing Reflection

Machiavelli's genius lay not simply in conquering territory, but in holding it with systems flexible enough to bend under strain yet rigid where principle demanded. Scaling your real-estate empire works the same: tighten leverage where revenue stutters; drill wargames until every shock is mapped; dispatch viceroys branded with your ethos but freed to maneuver; and call an orderly halt the instant early-warning dials flicker. Do so and growth becomes an accordion—expanding during windows of opportunity, contracting into fortified resilience when fortune churns—never a balloon waiting to pop. That rhythmic discipline, executed decade upon decade, is how empires leave stone footprints where rival kingdoms fade into dust.

Chapter 12: Innovation and Expansion—Strategic Growth Moves

Machiavelli on Bold, Timely Campaigns for Greater Power

Niccolò Machiavelli's *The Prince* resounds with a singular imperative: to grasp opportunity with audacity. He exhorts that "fortune favors the bold," urging rulers to strike decisively when the moment is ripe, rather than cling to safe but stagnant positions. In acquisition and post-close stewardship, this translates into seizing growth avenues swiftly—before competitors adapt or markets evolve.

Machiavelli warns that "whosoever desires constant success must change his conduct with the times," underscoring the perils of complacency. A market-leading product today can become tomorrow's relic if you fail to innovate. For the acquirer, the consolidation of a new business is only the prelude: the true test lies in expanding its reach, offerings, and technological foundations to secure enduring dominance.

He also counsels discernment: boldness without intelligence courts disaster. "He who is highly esteemed is not easily conspired against," Machiavelli observes, pointing out that well-timed, well-executed campaigns enhance reputation, whereas ill-judged expeditions foment resistance. You must therefore align your expansion moves with both internal strengths—your "armed forces"—and external signals, much as a prince chooses the precise hour to lead his army into battle.

New Product Lines, Geographic Branches, Digital Transformation

New Product Lines
 Building upon your acquired business's core competencies, branching into adjacent products can capture incremental share and deepen customer relationships. Machiavelli likens a prince's realm to a living organism: "Just as a tree sends forth branches and roots to strengthen its trunk, so must a principality extend outward to reinforce its center." In practice, analyze your customer base to identify unmet needs. If you lead a specialized manufacturing firm, could you introduce service contracts, parts kits, or training programs? If you run a B2B software company, consider modules or integrations that address emerging workflows.

- **Ideation Process**: Convene cross-functional teams—sales, R&D, customer support—to brainstorm complementary offerings. Draw upon frontline insights: customers often suggest features that solve their real-world pain points.

- **Rapid Prototyping**: Develop minimum-viable versions of two or three top concepts. Offer them to a small cohort of clients at discounted rates in exchange for candid feedback.

- **Launch Cadence**: Time product announcements to coincide with industry events or seasonal buying patterns, maximizing visibility and perceived momentum.

Geographic Branches

Markets vary by region: cultural preferences, regulatory regimes, distribution infrastructures. Machiavelli reminds princes that "different provinces require different modes of administration," and that successful emperors adapt to local customs. Accordingly, expansion into new territories demands careful localization.

- **Market Assessment**: For each potential region, conduct a PESTEL analysis—Political, Economic, Social, Technological, Environmental, Legal—to gauge entry viability.

- **Entry Models**: Decide between greenfield investments, joint ventures with local partners, or acquisition of smaller incumbents whose networks you can absorb. Each approach balances speed, cost, and risk.

- **Local Leadership**: Appoint managerial talent steeped in regional norms, thereby avoiding cultural missteps and building community trust. As Machiavelli noted, a ruler seen as an outsider must rely on native deputies to secure popular support.

Digital Transformation

In Machiavelli's age, princes who harnessed new military technologies—like artillery—surpassed rivals. Today, digital transformation is your equivalent artillery. Whether through automating workflows, migrating to cloud platforms, or deploying data-driven marketing, digital initiatives can multiply efficiency and customer reach.

- **Technology Audit**: Map your current digital stack—ERP, CRM, e-commerce, analytics—and identify gaps or legacy bottlenecks.

- **Digital Roadmap**: Prioritize projects with high value-at-stake: real-time inventory tracking to reduce stockouts, AI-driven customer support bots to enhance satisfaction, or omnichannel storefronts to capture mobile buyers.

- **Change Management**: Machiavelli warns against top-down edicts that ignore local realities. Pair every tech rollout with comprehensive training, clear communication of benefits, and pilot user groups to refine features before broad deployment.

Evaluating ROI: Pilot Programs vs. Full-Scale Rollouts

Machiavelli would disapprove of campaigns undertaken without reconnaissance. In growth initiatives, pilot programs serve as your scouts—small incursions that test assumptions before committing major resources.

Pilot Programs

- **Scope**: Limit pilots to a single product line, region, or customer segment. Define clear objectives—20 percent increase in trial conversions, 30 percent reduction in delivery errors, or positive net-promoter-score bump.

- **Duration & Budget**: Cap pilot efforts at 30–60 days and allocate no more than 5–10 percent of the total project budget. Machiavelli's princely advisors would counsel that modest initial commitments preserve strategic flexibility.

- **Evaluation Metrics**: Use quantitative KPIs (revenue lift, cost savings) and qualitative feedback (customer interviews, employee surveys) to assess feasibility. Only pilots meeting predefined success thresholds earn the green light for scale.

Full-Scale Rollouts

Once a pilot proves its concept, transition to enterprise deployment with confidence. However, Machiavelli warns against precipitous leaps: "One must remain cautious even in victory." For rollouts:

- **Phased Implementation**: Expand in waves—first to 10 percent, then 30 percent, finally 100 percent of the target audience—allowing mid-course corrections.

- **Resource Alignment**: Secure sufficient manpower, capital, and technology capacity before scaling. Avoid overwhelming your organization, which Machiavelli would liken to a fortress left understaffed after victory.

- **Governance Structure**: Establish a Growth Steering Committee to oversee rollout metrics, budget adherence, and issue resolution, meeting frequently during the initial phases and tapering cadence as stability emerges.

By calibrating your growth moves through pilots and phased rollouts, you heed Machiavelli's counsel to balance boldness with prudence—securing the spoils of conquest without destabilizing your realm.

Action Steps: Growth-Initiative Scoring; Pilot Launch Roadmap

Growth-Initiative Scoring
Develop a transparent rubric to prioritize potential expansion projects. Score each initiative on:

- **Strategic Alignment (1–5)**: How directly does the initiative support long-term goals?

- **Value-at-Stake (1–5)**: Estimated incremental revenue or cost savings.

- **Ease of Implementation (1–5)**: Resource requirements, technical complexity, and organizational readiness.

- **Risk Profile (1–5)**: Legal, operational, and market risks identified during pilots or due diligence.

Multiply scores to yield a priority index, then rank initiatives accordingly. Machiavelli favored data-driven counsel: this scoring ensures you commit to the boldest, most impactful campaigns first.

Pilot Launch Roadmap

1. **Project Charter**: Define scope, objectives, stakeholders, and success criteria.

2. **Team Assembly**: Assign a pilot leader, cross-functional team members, and executive sponsors.

3. **Timeline & Milestones**: Map key deliverables—prototype development, pilot launch, mid-pilot review, pilot close.

4. **Budget & Resources**: Secure funding, allocate personnel hours, and procure necessary tools or external partners.

5. **Communication Plan**: Announce the pilot internally and, if customer-facing, externally to the selected cohort.

6. **Data Collection Framework**: Set up dashboards, surveys, and feedback channels to capture quantitative and qualitative metrics.

7. **Mid-Pilot Review**: At halfway point, convene stakeholders to assess progress against success criteria and decide to pivot, persevere, or proceed to rollout.

8. **Pilot Conclusion & Analysis**: Compile results, lessons learned, and recommendations. Present findings to the Growth Steering Committee.

9. **Scale-Up Plan**: For successful pilots, detail phased rollout steps—additional funding, training programs, updated SOPs.

By following a disciplined pilot roadmap, you enact Machiavelli's principle that "counsel must be taken from the old and experienced," using real-world data before full-scale strategies.

Conclusion

In sum, strategic growth for your newly acquired business requires the audacity to pursue bold initiatives, the sagacity to pilot before scaling, and the discipline to score and govern every project. Through new product lines, geographic expansions, and digital transformations—all evaluated with Machiavelli's blend of bravery and calculation—you secure not just short-term triumphs, but long-lasting dominion in your industry principality.

Chapter 13 – Twenty-One Tactical Maxims for Everyday Decisions

Below are twenty-one field rules you can lift straight out of *The Prince* and slam onto your real-estate dashboard tomorrow morning. Each "law" carries three parts: a streamlined version of Machiavelli's line, a live-ammo scenario, and a precise action with a single KPI that tells you if the lesson is sticking.

---

1. **Law of the First Stone**
    Paraphrase: Strike hard at the outset; lingering doubts grow claws.
    Scenario: You inherit a property with month-to-month holdovers who pay late.
    Action & KPI: Issue immediate 30-day renew-or-vacate notices paired with online-only rent collection. Track "late payments per month." Goal: below 2 percent by the second billing cycle.

2. **Law of the Visible Sword**
    Paraphrase: Better feared than loved—provided fear never turns to hate.
    Scenario: Contractor misses milestones twice.
    Action & KPI: Enforce liquidated damages clause publicly but offer a performance bonus if the schedule recovers. Monitor "days behind schedule." Target: back on timeline within 14 days.

3. **Law of Earned Mercy**
    Paraphrase: Occasional generosity magnifies power when it's rare.
    Scenario: Tenant loses job; eviction looms.
    Action & KPI: Approve a one-time payment plan tied to job-placement proof. Measure "repayment completion rate." Success threshold: 90 percent.

4. **Law of the Steady Tribute**
    Paraphrase: People forget favors faster than tax hikes—keep revenue predictable.
    Scenario: Considering variable parking fees.
    Action & KPI: Switch to flat monthly parking rent with annual CPI bumps. Watch "parking-revenue variance." Aim for <3 percent swing YOY.

5. **Law of the Two Frontiers**
    Paraphrase: Guard borders you can reach; sell the rest.
    Scenario: Portfolio sprawls across five states.
    Action & KPI: Off-load the most remote 10 percent of units. Track "average miles per asset from regional office." Bring below 90-mile radius.

6. **Law of the Missing Middle**
    Paraphrase: Extremes of generosity or cruelty backfire; hit the median.
    Scenario: Debating rent increase size.
    Action & KPI: Raise rent one point below market, bundle free Wi-Fi. Measure "renewal percentage." Goal: ≥65 percent.

7. **Law of Forward Credit**

  Paraphrase: Spend reputation like gold—slowly and only on essentials.

  Scenario: City asks you to sponsor a gala.

  Action & KPI: Accept but negotiate naming-rights banner. Track "earned media mentions." Target: 5 positive hits.

8. **Law of Borrowed Blades**

  Paraphrase: Let others do the dirty work when legality allows.

  Scenario: Neighboring lot owner stores junk hurting curb appeal.

  Action & KPI: Submit code-violation photos to city; avoid personal dispute. Watch "days to violation correction." Success within 30 days.

9. **Law of Early Numbers**

  Paraphrase: Take the battlefield before opponents arrive.

  Scenario: Off-market lead whispers at 4 p.m. Friday.

  Action & KPI: Underwrite same day, LOI by Monday morning. KPI: "hours from lead to LOI"—target <72.

10. **Law of the Open Ledger**

  Paraphrase: Transparency disarms suspicious allies.

  Scenario: Private-equity partner skeptical of rehab budget.

  Action & KPI: Provide live Google-Sheet cost tracker with weekly auto-emails. KPI: "number of partner info requests." Target: cut by 75 percent.

11. **Law of the Double Lock**

  Paraphrase: Divide powers so no single guard controls both keys.

Scenario: Property manager approves invoices and pays vendors.
Action & KPI: Split duties; accounting must countersign. KPI: "unauthorized payment incidents." Goal: zero.

12. **Law of the Quiet Spy**
Paraphrase: Knowledge ahead of time equals victory without battle.
Scenario: Rumor of competitor buying three blocks down.
Action & KPI: Set county-transfer alerts; bid adjacent parcel first. KPI: "days from rival filing to your offer." Goal: <7.

13. **Law of the Scorched Checkbook**
Paraphrase: One brutal correction beats many small nicks.
Scenario: Vendor repeatedly overcharges micro amounts.
Action & KPI: Terminate contract, onboard new firm in one week. Measure "service-interruption hours." Target:≤4.

14. **Law of the Credible Exit**
Paraphrase: Always hold a door you can walk through.
Scenario: Negotiations stalling with seller demanding premium.
Action & KPI: Line up alternate property, mention progress. KPI: "price concession achieved." Goal: ≥5 percent drop.

15. **Law of Shared Spoils**
Paraphrase: Partners stay loyal when upside tastes sweet.
Scenario: Regional viceroy surpasses NOI.

Action & KPI: Pay 10 percent of excess as bonus. KPI: "viceroy retention rate." Aim: 100 percent yearly.

16. **Law of the Fixed Standard**
    Paraphrase: Changing laws mid-game breeds revolt.
    Scenario: New pet policy under debate.
    Action & KPI: Grandfather existing pets, apply rule only to new leases. KPI: "tenant complaints filed." Target: <3 first quarter.

17. **Law of the Off-Season Drill**
    Paraphrase: Train in peace to bleed less in war.
    Scenario: Slow leasing winter months.
    Action & KPI: Run fire-evacuation rehearsal and cybersecurity tabletop. KPI: "response-time improvement." Seek 25 percent faster.

18. **Law of Calculated Silence**
    Paraphrase: Say little; let results speak.
    Scenario: Social media claims slumlord behavior.
    Action & KPI: Post renovation before/after photos without addressing trolls directly. KPI: "positive comment ratio." Goal: 4:1 within two weeks.

19. **Law of Prepaid Trust**
    Paraphrase: Lend small sums before you need large favors.
    Scenario: Building inspector often nitpicks.
    Action & KPI: Offer conference room for city training session gratis. KPI: "average inspection write-ups." Reduce by half.

20. **Law of the Measured Retreat**
  Paraphrase: Exit with dignity before fortune demands exile.
  Scenario: Flagship asset's IRR falls under target.
  Action & KPI: List property at whisper price; start refi as fallback. KPI: "days on market to contract." Target ≤30 while DSCR≥1.30.

21. **Law of the Aging Prince**
  Paraphrase: Build heirs while muscles still flex.
  Scenario: Founder hits age 60; no succession.
  Action & KPI: Enroll chosen protégé in 18-month shadow program. KPI: "competency score on quarterly board review." Must reach 90/100 by graduation.

Put these maxims where you log rent rolls. Review them like weight-room fundamentals—because in property, as in politics, the daily reps decide who stands tall when the towers and page views fade. Machiavelli handed you the playbook; your KPIs will tell you whether you're actually running the plays.

THIS IS NOT A COLLECTION

This volume is part of **Ancient Wisdom Hacks**—
an ongoing body of work focused on how strategy, power, and
failure actually function under pressure.

The books are only one layer.

What you are reading is an entry point into a larger system of
interpretation, application, and expansion.

WHAT THESE WORKS ARE DESIGNED TO DO

Most people look for answers.

These works expose patterns:

- How decisions are made before they are visible
- How systems weaken before they collapse
- How power shifts before it is recognized

This is not theory.
It is applied observation.

THE SYSTEM BEHIND THE WORK

Across all volumes and future releases, three forces remain
constant:

- **Strategy** — how outcomes are shaped before action
- **Conflict** — how people and systems break under pressure
- **Power** — how control is gained, maintained, and lost

No single book contains the full picture.
Each adds another angle.

CONTINUE BEYOND THIS VOLUME

New interpretations, applied volumes, and extended works are
released continuously.

To access current and future material, visit:

www.AncientWisdomHacks.com

WHAT YOU WILL FIND

- Additional applied volumes across industries
- Expanded interpretations of foundational texts
- New releases not available through standard distribution
- Future projects extending beyond books

The system is still expanding.

FINAL POSITION

Clarity does not make outcomes easier.

It removes the illusion that they were ever simple.

Ancient Wisdom Hacks
Interpretation over repetition.
Application over theory.